Nicole Wilde, CPDT

Getting a Grip on Aggression Cases

Practical Considerations for Dog Trainers

Phantom Publishing

Getting a Grip on Aggression Cases:
Practical Considerations for Dog Trainers
by Nicole Wilde, CPDT

Copyright © 2008 by Nicole Wilde

Published by:
Phantom Publishing
P.O. Box 2814
Santa Clarita, CA 91386
www.phantompub.com

First Edition

ISBN 978-0-9817227-1-9

Photo credits:
Cover photo: Kimberly Warner
p.72 photo #2 Mychelle Blake
p.73 Laura Bourhenne
pp. 171 & 172 Stephanie Coleman
Photos pp. 69, 71 and dedication page by the author.

For Mojo

Other books by Nicole Wilde:

Living with Wolfdogs

Wolfdogs A-Z: Behavior, Training & More

So You Want to be a Dog Trainer

It's Not the Dogs, It's the People! A Dog Trainer's Guide to Training Humans (book, audio CD)

One on One: A Dog Trainer's Guide to Private Lessons

Help for Your Fearful Dog

Throughout this book, in most cases, dogs are referred to as male and owners as female. This is simply for ease of reading and implies no gender bias.

Acknowledgements

As always, I owe a huge debt of gratitude to Ian Dunbar, without whose encouragement there never would have been a first book, never mind a seventh. Thank you, Ian, for your generosity, your friendship, and for being such an amazing human being. The dog training world is incredibly fortunate to have you.

To my editor Leslie Bockian, you surely deserve some sort of award (perhaps a Silver Semi-Colon Statuette?), not only for editing this book, but for making what can be a grueling process into something fun. Thank you for your friendship, your encouragement, the silly dog cartoons, and most of all, your warped sense of humor.

Thanks to Mychelle Blake for taking the time to read over the manuscript and make suggestions, despite your insanely busy schedule. And while I'm at it, thanks for designing the Phantom Publishing website. You get more done in a day than most people do in a week, and still somehow manage to do an excellent job. You rock!

Paul Owens, the *original* Dog Whisperer, thank you for your input, and for continuing to be a voice for non-violent dog training.

James O'Heare, thank you for supplying studies and never making me feel that I was being a pest!

Dr. Sabine Hellge, thank you for the research study and translation.

To my husband C.C., thank you for always encouraging me and being, in your words, my "biggest fan." Your love and support mean more to me than I can say. I'm so blessed to have you as a friend and life partner.

Last but definitely not least, I am indebted to all the dogs and wolves I have worked with over the years who have taught me so much about behavior issues. I am especially grateful to Mojo, who I made my mistakes with and learned so much from, and who is and always will be my "soul dog."

Table of Contents

Part III   The Session

Part IV   What Do I Do If...

Introduction

Aggression. The very word sends tingles up the spine of many a dog trainer. Some practically bristle with excitement at the opportunity to work with a dog who is beginning to show signs of aggression, or who has already bitten. While that might sound odd, it can be incredibly fulfilling to see a dog transform from a feared, ostracized, "problem dog" who is in danger of losing his home into a trusted and treasured family member. Bringing about a major turnaround in a dog's behavior, making a meaningful impact on the lives of dogs and their owners and, at times, helping to make the difference between life or death for a dog, can be thrilling. Working with aggressive dogs can be enormously rewarding on an emotional level as well as a financial one.

Other trainers recoil at the thought of dealing with aggression on any level. They do not understand why anyone would ever choose to work with a dog who might bite! That's perfectly understandable. Dog bites hurt, and aggressive behavior can be frightening. I know many trainers who do not accept aggression cases, don't ever plan to, and still have satisfying, flourishing careers.

There are also a number of trainers who are in a sort of limbo: they would like to start working with aggression issues but aren't quite sure how to go about it. Perhaps you, like so many others, have mastered the art of teaching obedience skills and working with behavior issues, but have not yet had the experience of working with dogs who display aggressive behavior. Without having interned with another trainer or at least having had the opportunity to observe these types of sessions, it can be difficult to know how to proceed, and downright confusing to figure out how to conduct a session. I remember wondering early in my career just how the heck a trainer was supposed to even *be* in the same room as a dog who was aggressive toward people, never mind train him!

I have been working with aggressive dogs for over fifteen years now. There have been many who were aggressive toward unfamiliar dogs (although some turned out to be more what I would term "dog-obnoxious"—bullies—than truly dangerous). Others had "possession aggression." (No, the dogs weren't levitating or spitting up green pea soup—they had resource guarding issues involving valued items, locations, or even family members.) As it happens, the majority of cases I see involve aggression toward people. The dogs have ranged from conflicted adolescents who were testing their newfound bravado to confident adults who had inflicted multiple puncture wounds on multiple people.

Whether you are currently undecided as to whether you would like to work with aggressive dogs, have already made the decision but are not quite sure how to get started, or are already experienced at handling aggression cases, you will find this book extremely helpful. We'll begin with a discussion of the definition, levels, and types of aggression. Next, we'll explore the topics of liability, insurance, and maintaining personal safety at sessions. Then we'll really "get a grip" on aggression cases: specific training equipment, secrets of taking a thorough history, and how to structure sessions. You will find questionnaires that are specific to individual types of aggression issues, and a more generalized one for taking a bite history. There are questions to add to your existing behavioral intake forms, a format for follow-up letters to be sent to veterinarians, considerations to help determine whether your liability contract is iron-clad, and valuable tips on how to handle dogs and clients more effectively.

You will get straightforward, concrete answers to questions that most trainers have, such as how and when to recommend rehoming or euthanasia, how to handle reactive dogs in group classes, and what to do if you are bitten at a session. An entire chapter is dedicated to the vital topic of how to break up a dog fight. You will also hear stories from my own professional practice throughout the book.

Your compassion and desire to help dogs who have aggression issues, combined with the knowledge you will acquire here, will surely contribute to making a positive difference in the lives of countless dogs and people.

Part I

Overview
&
Practical
Considerations

What is Aggression?

Susan sounds frazzled. She is calling, she says, because she has reached the end of her rope:

> *"Jasper is so out of control. He's really aggressive!"*

> *"Can you explain what you mean by 'aggressive'?" I respond. What's Jasper doing, exactly?"*

> *"Well, he jumps on the kids and grabs at their clothing. If my two-year-old has food in his hand, Jasper will jump up and grab it away from him." Susan finishes by reemphasizing, "He's only six months old, but he's really aggressive!"*

While it's true that Jasper's behavior is troublesome, and probably not much fun to live with, it is far from being aggressive. Susan's description is actually fairly typical of a boundary-pushing, selective-hearing adolescent who lacks proper manners and perhaps sufficient exercise, mental stimulation, and strong leadership. It's no surprise that Jasper keeps trying to get what he wants through sheer physical force; it works. But the distinction is important: although Jasper's behavior may be obnoxious, it is not aggressive.

~ * ~ * ~ *~ * ~ * ~ *~ * ~ * ~ *~ * ~ * ~ *

A local rescue group recently adopted out Jojo, a two-year-old Labrador retriever mix, to first-time dog owners Claire and Andy. The couple felt that a friendly canine companion would be just the thing to help four-year-old Robby overcome his fear of dogs. Unfortunately, within the first week of being in his new home, Jojo bit Robby on the leg, breaking the skin and leaving Robby terrified. Jojo also bit Andy, leaving large, ugly bruises on his forearm. The whole family, Claire confided to me on the phone, was afraid of the dog. After a lengthy discussion, I advised Claire that while she could certainly employ my services to evaluate Jojo, she would be better off returning him to the rescue immediately, as the safety and emotional well-being of her child was paramount. Claire agreed. But when she informed the rescue group of her intentions, they convinced her to have their trainer come out to see her instead, as they felt that Jojo was not at all aggressive, but rather, simply in need of training.

After the trainer's visit, Claire phoned me. She was obviously distraught. The trainer, in addition to informing Claire that the dog was "stubborn," "emotionally manipulative," and a number of other adjectives that would have been better suited to describe a human being, told her in no uncertain terms that, "Unless a dog draws blood, it's not aggressive." Fortunately, Claire eventually convinced the group to take Jojo back.

~ * ~ * ~ *~ * ~ * ~ *~ * ~ * ~ *~ * ~ * ~ *

What the parties involved in both stories have in common is an unrealistic view of what the term "aggression" means. Put as simply as possible, *aggression is an intent to cause harm.* A dog who lunges at a person who enters the back yard and sinks his teeth repeatedly into the person's leg is most certainly displaying aggression, most likely of a territorial nature. A dog who knocks children over during play, jumps on visitors, nips when excited, or wrestles with other dogs in an overly rough manner is surely in need of training—but the behavior is not actually aggressive.

The Baby, the Bathwater, and Buddy's Behavior

There are some dogs any knowledgeable trainer would classify as having severe aggression issues. If Spike bit the last five people who walked through the front door, there is no argument that there is a serious problem. But things are not always so cut and dried. For example, Buddy has bitten two other dogs at the park. You might be tempted to label Buddy as "aggressive." But what if I told you that each bite had been triggered by the other dog acting in a threatening manner and, as Buddy was on leash at the time, he had no way to retreat? That certainly changes the picture, doesn't it?

If Fifi is the epitome of Miss Canine Congeniality in everyday life, but snaps at the vet tech whenever she gets vaccinated, is Fifi an "aggressive" dog? The tech might think so, but he is only seeing Fifi in one context. There is a difference between stating that a dog displays aggressive behavior in particular situations or even that a dog has "aggressive tendencies," and labeling that dog as "aggressive." The latter should be avoided.

Let's look at a human example. Imagine a day when you are not at your best. Perhaps you had a long, frustrating morning at work, aren't feeling well, and are just plain grouchy. As a result, after standing in line at the store for thirty minutes on your lunch break to return a purchase, you blow up at the customer service person. The poor man, who was having a decent enough day until his innocent inquiry about your item resulted in a hailstorm of verbal darts, forms an instant opinion of you—one that involves a word used to describe female dogs. The man now sees you as a person with a short temper, and one he would prefer not to deal with in the future. Based on that one encounter, you have been labeled as having a specific personality type. Now, you and I know that on most days, you are a perfectly nice, pleasant person. But on that day, you were acting in a distinctly unpleasant manner. Was the label applied to you fair and accurate in general?

Throughout this book, whenever you see the terms "aggressive," "reactive" (reacting to something by barking, lunging, or displaying other threatening behavior, but not biting), or "fear-reactive" (the reactive behavior is fear-based), they are meant to describe a dog's behavior in a specific situation rather than the dog's temperament in general. It may well be that the dog in question is one trainers would evaluate as "aggressive," but discussing behavior in specific contexts rather than making broad generalizations is more scientifically accurate as well as more constructive.

Discussing Aggression with Clients

Discussing aggressive behavior in precise terms is especially important when speaking with clients. It is important to be compassionate, but you must also be straightforward regarding the severity of a dog's issues. There is no need to be politically correct: "I'm sorry, ma'am, but your dog seems to be friendliness-challenged!" If a dog is truly dangerous, say so.

Be careful not to label a dog who displays aggressive behavior in particular circumstances as aggressive across the board. Doing so would only give the owner, who is already distressed at the dog's behavior, one more reason to view the dog in a negative light; that could, in turn, lead to behavior on the owner's part that exacerbates the problem.

Imagine that Lisa solicits your services because Hutch, her year-old border collie mix, bit another dog. It is the first time he has ever bitten anyone, canine or human. You visit the home and explain to Lisa that Hutch is dog-aggressive. As a result of your assertion, whenever Hutch is around other dogs, Lisa becomes nervous; she has been informed by a *professional*, after all, that Hutch is aggressive. She assumes that Hutch has all the personality traits that, to her mind, accompany the label: "not to be trusted;" "unpredictable;" "dangerous;" and others. The nervous disposition of his owner around other dogs makes Hutch even more nervous, which causes further problems.

Now imagine instead that you explain to Lisa that Hutch is a sweet, intelligent, lovely dog. This one incident, which will certainly be taken seriously and addressed in depth, does not make Hutch a "bad dog" overall. You will work together to identify what triggers his behavior, and will keep other dogs safe as you go about resolving the problem. Now you have an owner with a completely different outlook. Lisa's positive feelings toward Hutch remain intact, and she feels optimistic that his behavior can be modified.

Evaluating and treating canine aggression is both an art and a science. The art of intuiting which methods or treatments will work for a particular dog, and correctly assessing behavior, is developed through experience. The scientific aspect will be addressed next, beginning with the definition and categorization of aggresion levels.

2

Levels of Aggression

In many cases, whether or not a dog intends harm is obvious. However, displays of aggressive behavior are not all the same in intensity or intent; they fall on a continuum. At the mild end, a dog may give a hard stare, raise hackles, bare teeth, growl, or air snap. Those signals are warnings that a bite may follow, rather than being aggressive acts in and of themselves. If heeded, the signals actually serve to *avoid* aggression. If a child approaches a dog who is guarding his food, the dog growls, and the child retreats, a bite has been averted. If a dog freezes in place, lowers his head and stares at another dog, it is a warning to that dog to back off. The posturing is a communication, not an act of violence.

Continuing along the spectrum, we find dogs whose teeth are contacting skin, whether of other dogs or people. At the mild end is a tentative approach where the dog darts in, makes contact, and retreats. This may involve a nip or a "muzzle punch," a closed-mouth jab that is often indicative of testing behavior. If a bite is inflicted, although it might hurt, it does not break the skin. This is the type of bite that is often delivered by an adolescent dog who is just starting to gain confidence and test his power.

We see this kind of behavior too from dogs who are fearful, as an attempt to increase the distance between them and the dog or person they feel threatened by. If the dog learns that it works, the result may be increasingly more confident bites as time goes on. The quick, tentative bite is normally that of a dog who does not have an extensive bite history, and at this level, the bite is not intended so much to cause harm as it is to cause the recipient to retreat.

> Any dog, if feeling threatened enough, may bite.

Now we come to more confident bites. The dog who lunges at another dog or person and bites in a self-assured manner has very likely had practice. The confident bite may be delivered when a stranger enters the home or yard, when someone attempts to take something from the dog, when another dog is encountered, or in a variety of other circumstances. This type of bite is intended to deliver a message! That message may be read on the skin in the form of bruising or bite marks. At this level the dog bites, then disengages. The bite may or may not be preceded by a warning; if a dog has been punished for growling in the past, the dog might now bite without giving any warning signals at all.

Crossing the line from a bite to an attack, we find deeper bites and multiple bites. This behavior falls into the category of severe aggression and should be taken extremely seriously. It is one thing for a dog to bite lightly and release in order to express his displeasure at having his toenails clipped, and quite another to launch himself at the groomer's arm, leaving multiple puncture wounds.

Even more severe is the behavior of the dog who sinks teeth deep into flesh, and rather than releasing, holds on and shakes it from side to side the way a dog would shake another animal to kill it. Fortunately, the vast majority of aggression cases that trainers are called in to work with do not fall on the extreme end of the spectrum.

A 1991 study suggests that male dogs are 6.2 times as likely to bite as female dogs.[1] Males are more likely to fight with other males, and females with females. The chances of aggression are highest among same-sex siblings.

Bite Levels

Renowned author, veterinarian and animal behaviorist Ian Dunbar has devised a scale for assessing the severity of a bite. The scale is a useful tool to categorize bite levels, and to allow for a mutual understanding of terms when discussing aggression cases with other trainers.

Level One	Bark, lunge, air-snap. No teeth touching skin.
Level Two	Teeth touch skin, possible scrapes or welts, but no puncture.
Level Three	One to four holes from a single bite. All holes less than half the length of a single canine tooth; sometimes a tear.
Level Four	One to four holes deeper than half the length of a canine tooth (dog bit and clamped down); possible deep black bruising within 24 hours; and/or rips in both directions (dog bit and shook his head).
Level Five	Multiple bite attack with deep punctures, or multiple attacks. Rips in both directions, vast amounts of flesh damaged. (These are the type of bites that hospitalize and sometimes kill people.)
Level Six	Killed victim and/or consumed flesh.

Level one and two displays are, unfortunately, often ignored until a more severe incident has taken place. It should also be noted that a level two bite, although it technically does not puncture the skin, can still cause damage. Canine jaws are incredibly strong (an average German shepherd applies 750 pounds of pressure per square inch), and can easily crush tissue and cause bruising without ever piercing the skin. But level one and *mild* level two bite cases are relatively safe to work with, and normally have a good prognosis.

Many rescue groups and shelters will not place dogs with a bite history of level three and over, or will not place them into homes with small children—and rightly so. If a dog is delivering level three bites or above in a home environment, his actions are usually troubling enough for the family to call a trainer. You should only take on level three bites if you have the necessary experience and expertise, as well as complete owner compliance.

Level four bites are very serious and intense, and should be addressed as such. Dogs in this category either have a serious lack of bite inhibition or, more likely, are confident, experienced biters. Some trainers will accept cases that involve level four and even level five bites. In the category of level five biters are dogs who have inflicted multiple puncture wounds on multiple people or dogs. These bites most definitely imply a more serious problem than a lack of bite inhibition. Obviously, the cautions about working with level three biters apply here as well. At this level, you should be aware that your discussion with the client will probably include the topics of management and/or euthanasia.

Dogs who administer level six bites are almost always euthanized, as they pose a severe and potentially deadly threat. These are the dogs you hear about on the news who have mauled a child or sometimes an adult, and about whom behaviorists are called in to testify in court. Again, the chances that you will run into this level of aggressive behavior in your practice are very slim.

1 Gershman KA, Sacks JJ, Wright JC. Which dogs bite? A case-control study of risk factors. *Pediatrics* 1994; 93:913-917

Types of Aggression

Offensive or Defensive?

Most displays of aggression can be described as either *offensive* or *defensive*. A defensive display is the result of a dog feeling threatened. For example, a dog who is subjected to repeated rough jerks on a choke chain by a trainer finally bites. Another example would be a dog who bites when someone reaches to pet him on his arthritic, painful hindquarters. With defensive aggression, the dog truly feels he has no other choice; it's that old fight-or-flight instinct, and in this case, the fight response is engaged.

With offensive aggression, the dog takes the lead. For example, a dog who is territorial may run across the yard, jump up at the fence, and bite a stranger who tries to enter the property. A dog who runs at and attacks other dogs with little provocation is demonstrating offensive aggression as well.

Common Types of Aggression

Listed below are common types of aggression you are likely to encounter. Some, such as dog-dog and dog-human, may be either offensive or defensive. Others, like predatory aggression and territorial aggression, are always offensive. Handling issues and medically-related issues are normally defensive.

Dog-dog aggression: May be aimed at all other dogs, unfamiliar dogs only, or at another dog in the home.

Aggression toward people: May be aimed at one or more family members (sometimes termed "dominance aggression") or at unfamiliar people.

Resource guarding: Zealously protecting food, treats, toys, locations, people, or just about anything—some dogs have even been known to guard things as insignificant as lint!

Territorial aggression: This is actually a form of resource guarding, as the dog is defending what he perceives to be his. Dogs may become territorial over the back yard, the home, the area in front of the house, or a familiar walking route.

Predatory aggression: The chase drive that is instinctive to all dogs becomes problematic when the end result is damage to another animal or person. For example, many dogs chase and injure cats.

Handling issues: These may include having nails clipped, being brushed or bathed, being petted or handled in a certain way or on a particular area of the body (a red flag that the dog may be in pain), or being picked up or moved.

Redirected aggression: This behavior can occur when a dog is in an aroused state; although the focus of his aggression is another dog or person, he "redirects" and bites the nearest person (usually the owner) instead. Redirected aggression is common when trying to separate fighting dogs; the dogs are so worked up that they see the interceding hand or limb as an intrusion, and snap at it.

Dogs may redirect on to each other as well. For example, two dogs in a back yard who are running the length of a chain link fence together, barking at a dog on the other side, may eventually become so agitated that they turn on each other. Two dogs walking together may become so aroused at the sight of another dog that, being restrained on leashes, they become reactive toward each other (an excellent argument against the use of couplers—products that allow two dogs to be walked with one leash).

Medically-related aggression: This category covers any ailment, injury, disease, or other physical malady that is causing a dog to feel unwell, and therefore to act in an aggressive manner.

Trainer Sue Sternberg has stated that aggression normally happens in two common circumstances: when a dog is being stopped from doing something he wants to do, or an owner is trying to get a dog to do something he does not want to do. I agree wholeheartedly. For example, I have heard of many an owner being bitten when trying to load the dog into a vehicle or crate into which the dog obviously did not want to go. You will find that many of the aggression issues you treat will fall into one of Sternberg's two categories, as well as falling into one or more of the classifications described in this chapter.

Case Selection and Education

The Case of the Overconfident Trainer

I recently received a request by a new trainer in my area to meet for lunch. When I say "new" I don't mean she was new to the area, but new to dog training. Cindy had trained her own dogs and a few friends' dogs, and was now advertising herself as a professional trainer. Now, you wouldn't hang out a shingle saying you are a children's teacher if your experience consisted of teaching your own kids and one or two friends' kids; it should be no different with dog training. Despite my conviction that trainers should have plenty of book learning and hands-on experience (and preferably have apprenticed with another trainer as well) before opening a business, I agreed to get together.

Over lunch, Cindy mentioned that she had an appointment scheduled the following week for a behavior consult with a woman whose dog was aggressive. I was more than a bit surprised that someone who had just started training would take on a case that involved aggression, and I politely said so. It wasn't a simple case, either, but a situation where two female dogs of the same age were fighting in the home. Cindy seemed unaware of the fact that female-female aggression, particularly between two dogs of the same age, can be an intensely serious situation. Despite my gentle attempt to encourage her to refer the woman to someone with more experience, and to perhaps tag along on the session as a learning experience, she insisted on seeing the woman herself.

Cindy reported back after the session. She'd spent upwards of two hours with the woman. I asked how the lesson had gone and what had been accomplished. "Well," she announced proudly, "the one dog doesn't pull on the leash anymore. It's not good leadership to let your dog walk in front of you." When I asked how that related to the aggression issue in the home, she didn't have an answer. She did admit that once she realized she didn't know how to address the actual aggression issue, she had referred the woman to my training company.

Unfortunately, that woman never called. My guess is that she didn't call another trainer, either, having just spent quite a bit of money (Cindy was charging top rates). The unfortunate pairing of a very serious behavior issue with a trainer who was inexperienced and unable to help could literally have meant life or death for one of those dogs. For all I know, it did. Taking on aggression cases you are not equipped to deal with doesn't just affect *you* negatively—it can also have a huge impact on the dogs' chances of staying in the home, and sometimes, their survival.

Take It or Leave It

Which cases you accept should be based on your knowledge and comfort level in handling the specific type of aggression, and the intensity of the behavior. If you are confident working with dogs who have mild resource guarding issues, but not those who bite people, start there; accept the resource guarding cases and refer the others. Referring a client to another professional is not an admission of failure! On the contrary, saying that an issue is beyond your expertise is a sign of professionalism and sound ethics.

If you know of another trainer who is competent at handling aggression issues, refer the case. If you want to learn more about that type of aggression, ask whether you can go along on the session to observe. If the issue is one you feel may require medication or is beyond the level of expertise of your colleagues, refer the case to a Veterinary Behaviorist. Veterinary Behaviorists are not exactly plentiful, but some will work with your clients long-distance either directly or through their veterinarian. Another type of professional you can refer to is a Certified Applied Animal Behaviorist. (See *Resources*.)

Speaking of "behaviorists," some trainers use that title when advertising their services. While there is no law against a trainer advertising as a behaviorist, it is not recommended. If a lawsuit were to arise and you had advertised yourself as a behaviorist, you would be expected to perform the job at the level of someone who actually has that professional title. Unless you have the credential, if you want to advertise that you treat behavior issues, call yourself a behavior specialist or behavior consultant instead.

Should I Stay or Should I Go?

Referring a case during an initial phone inquiry is simple enough, but what if you're already at the session and find that the dog is more aggressive than originally represented? If the behavior is more intense than what you are comfortable handling, you can still refer the case out.

Early in my career, I went to see a new client who had an adult female Rhodesian ridgeback. The issue I was called in to address had nothing to do with aggression, nor was there any mention of it. As the owner and I stood in his kitchen, the brown 100-plus-pound dog wagged her tail and accepted petting from me with nice, loose body language, acting perfectly affectionate and friendly. Seconds later, she whipped around and sank her teeth into my forearm. (After all, if you're going to be bitten, why not by a breed designed to single-handedly bring down a lion!) Now, normally when someone says that a dog bit "without warning," the reality is that the person missed the dog's subtle warning signals. Although I had not done a lot of professional training at that point, I did have extensive experience in reading canine body language—my background involves working with rescued wolves and wolfdogs, who are great teachers of body language—and I was extremely careful about controlling my own movements. I had not made any sudden gestures or moved my hand to pet a different area of her body (one that might have been sensitive). To this day, that ridgeback was one of the few dogs I have seen who truly gave absolutely no warning signs.

The bite hurt my pride more than my arm. I was shaken, and told the man immediately that this was beyond my expertise and that I would refer him to another trainer. He convinced me to sit and chat for a few minutes, whereupon I discovered that the dog had a history of erratic behavior that included attempted and actual bites, as well as some medical issues. And she'd just come into heat, which probably didn't help matters. I felt embarrassed about the entire incident, regardless of the fact that it was not my fault. I did the right thing by referring the case out. Looking back more than fifteen years later, that was not an easy case, even for an experienced trainer.

Education

Are You Experienced?

At this point, you're probably wondering exactly how you're supposed to gain experience so you can feel comfortable taking on increasingly more intense cases, or what to do if you haven't handled aggression cases at all. The best way to learn is to be mentored by a professional trainer who has plenty of experience with aggression. If you can find this type of opportunity in your area, go for it! Being mentored one-on-one is the best educational experience you can get. Some trainers offer free internships (usually with the understanding that you will eventually work for their company), while others charge for their training programs. Either way, if you can mentor under an experienced trainer who uses sound, gentle training methods, it's a bargain and a good investment in your career.

Although I am not aware of any schools that focus solely on working hands-on with aggression issues, there are some train-the-trainer academies whose curriculums include the topic of aggression. On the west coast, the Marin Humane Society and the San Francisco SPCA are both good choices. For contact information for these and other schools and academies, see *Resources*.

If you don't have a mentorship or schooling opportunity in your area, you can still learn a great deal from reading books and attending seminars, and by participating in distance learning via the internet or telecourses (seminars conducted by phone). The Companion Animal Sciences Institute, founded by James O'Heare, offers an excellent online learning opportunity. The courses are well grounded in scientific theory, and are concentrated around learning theory and training issues. There is also a course that focuses specifically on aggressive canine behavior. Raising Canine offers telecourses on a variety of topics including aggression. (See *Resources* for information on both organizations.)

The Association of Pet Dog Trainers, commonly referred to as the APDT, is open to professional trainers and dog enthusiasts alike. This membership organization promotes dog-friendly training methods, and encourages networking through an online discussion list. Many experienced trainers participate, and you can get your questions answered by those who have been there and done that. The annual APDT conference, held in a different U.S. city each year, features some of the top names in canine training and behavior. Seminar topics range from basic information, such as learning theory for new trainers, to cutting-edge behavioral science. Offerings always include at least one or two excellent aggression-related presentations. There are also hands-on "wet labs" (not big soggy dogs, but hands-on training) and demonstrations, and the trade show features new products and training equipment. Audio recordings of conferences beginning in 2002 are available through Netsymposium (see *Resources*).

DVDs and Books

A wonderful way to check out seminars that are out of range either geographically or financially is to watch them on DVD. Tawzer Dog Videos stocks a multitude of excellent seminar DVDs on aggression topics. They offer a wide selection of presentations by some of the world's leading experts in canine behavior. I cannot say enough good things about the company, and I have ordered many of their DVDs myself over the years. Recommendations for specific titles are included in *Resources*.

Also included in the *Resources* section are books that specifically address the topic of aggression. Most, if not all, are available through Dogwise. Dogwise has long been a well-respected, leading distributor of canine-related books, many of which are geared toward trainers. This is another company that I, along with countless other trainers, depend on for the latest and greatest products. The company offers some excellent books on the topic of aggression, and has recently branched out to distribute DVDs as well.

Other Research Topics

There are topics that are not strictly aggression-related but are still worth investing some time to learn about, as they will help immensely in your work with aggressive dogs:

Breed characteristics. Understanding the characteristics and tendencies of individual breeds will help you to better assess aggression issues. For example, Siberian huskies have strong predatory instincts. If you get a call from a potential client with a husky who is actively stalking the family cat, the case may be challenging. While some breeds, such as beagles, are generally sociable with other dogs, others, such as Anatolian shepherds, tend not to accept unfamiliar dogs easily, making dog-dog aggression cases more difficult to resolve.

Some breeds naturally play more roughly than others. If you were not aware of a breed's tendency to put the "rough" in "roughhouse," you might mistake tough play for aggression. Certain breeds tend to be exuberantly mouthy—think retrievers—which can be mistaken for aggression. Others are aloof—Japanese breeds such as the Akita come to mind—which can be misinterpreted as well.

Shelter volunteering is a great way to get a feel for the tendencies of various breeds. Another is to visit breed rescue groups. If you call a local breed-specific rescue and say you are a trainer who would like a chance to discuss the breed so you can better help those you encounter, the person should be receptive. Ultimately, it will help to keep the dogs out of rescue! Besides, unlike some breeders who focus only on the positive aspects of the breed, a rescue person is likely to share the more challenging temperament traits as well.

The more you know about the characteristic behaviors of the breeds you encounter, the more effective you will be. If you have scheduled an appointment with a new client whose dog is a breed you are not very familiar with, do some research before the session. Recommended books and DVDs can be found in the *Resources* section.

Canine body language. It is crucial that you are able to recognize the differences between a fearful display, an aggressive display, and a dog who is conflicted and vacillating between the two. Volunteering at a shelter, humane society, or rescue group offers an excellent opportunity to get an overview of what various types of body language look like on different breeds. You'll find that some breeds, including those who normally have docked tails (for example, Rottweilers), are more challenging to read (for people *and* for other dogs). You will be privy to a non-stop parade of canine body language and interaction that no amount of book research can offer. Working with large numbers of dogs in a shelter or rescue environment will, over time, allow you to hone your instincts and develop a sort of sixth sense about temperament and the potential for aggression. That intuition will serve as one of your most valuable tools throughout your career. For books and DVDs on canine body language see *Resources*.

Years ago, I helped a fellow trainer to design a temperament testing program for a local shelter. Once our protocol had been established, the next step was to test it on some of the resident dogs. First, we walked down the long rows of pens to decide which dogs to use. We passed a pen that held a Rottweiler who immediately elicited the response from me, "Not that one!" although I couldn't tell you why. I'm quite fond of Rotties, especially large males, and this big, handsome boy wasn't doing anything that would normally set off a red flag. There was just something…not right. When we passed his pen again on our way back, he lunged at the bars, hitting them violently and repeatedly, assuring me in no uncertain terms that I had made the right decision. If the hairs on the back of your neck stand up, or you "just have a feeling," there is a good reason for it. *Listen to your instincts.* (An excellent book on this topic—non-dog-related but absolutely applicable—is Gavin DeBecker's *The Gift of Fear.*)

Learning theory. Some trainers are naturally talented at handling dogs, without ever having opened a book on learning theory. Others are well educated in book knowledge, but lack hands-on experience. The best trainers have both. Learn about classical and operant conditioning, desensitization and counterconditioning, and other principles that are vital to constructing well-designed protocols and understanding the psychological basis of canine behavior. Understanding the terminology will also allow you to have clearer communication when you discuss these issues with other professionals. For books and DVDs, see *Resources*.

Fear issues. As the vast majority of aggression issues are fear-based, it makes sense to have a good understanding of fear issues. Very often puppies who are fearful begin to demonstrate fear-based aggression when they hit adolescence and confidence grows. The more you know about fearful behavior, the better you can help owners to prevent it from turning into aggression, and to assist those who have sought help only after the fear-based behavior has become dangerous. My book *Help for Your Fearful Dog* is an extensive resource, and overlaps with the topic of fear-based aggression. For other helpful resources, you guessed it…see the *Resources* section.

Health and medical issues potentially related to aggression. Some health issues, such as thyroid imbalance, liver shunt, arthritis, ear infections, and other painful conditions can cause dogs to act in an aggressive manner. Even having been recently vaccinated can affect behavior. While you cannot legally dispense medical advice, knowing which physical causes might be underlying the behavior will allow you to suggest that the client discuss the matter with a veterinarian.

The topic of the influence of medical problems on aggressive behavior is a fascinating one, and could fill an entire book by itself. Do your research, as the more you understand about the possible causes of aggression, the better. Being knowledgeable on the subject will also save you from wasting your time attempting to treat a medically-based aggression issue with behavior modification alone. Another health-related topic to become familiar with is nutrition and how it affects canine behavior. Books on medical and nutritional links to aggression are included in *Resources*.

Complementary therapies. There are many therapies and remedies that can be useful when used in conjunction with behavior modification to treat aggression issues. These include the Anxiety Wrap, TTouch, Bach flower essences, homeopathy, herbal remedies, acupuncture, acupressure, DAP (Dog Appeasing Pheromone), and many more. You might not choose to use all of these modalities, but the more familiar you are with them, the more choices you will have in assisting your clients. And though you cannot offer veterinary advice, you should have a basic understanding of how, in some cases, pharmacological intervention can assist in behavior modification. That way, you can guide clients to discuss the topic with a veterinarian if you feel it is necessary.

The "Complementary Therapies" section of *Help for Your Fearful Dog* gives a brief overview of the aforementioned therapies and remedies. Other recommended books and DVDs are listed in the *Resources* section.

The sheer volume of knowledge required to work successfully with aggression cases might seem daunting, but it is reassuring to know that there are so many useful educational resources available. The bottom line is to take it slow. Learn as you go, and never take on any case that feels uncomfortable or overwhelming. As you gain experience, you will naturally take on more challenging cases. Should you decide to stay at the level you are at currently, that is a perfectly valid decision as well.

5

Legal Considerations

In 2000, a 45-year-old ex-firefighter named Gabriel Febbraio left his mother's home in Brooklyn, New York to go jogging. Realizing that he'd forgotten his gloves, he headed back to the house. It was at that point that he encountered Peter Borchelt, an author who holds a doctorate in animal behavior and is often called upon to testify in dog bite cases. Dr. Borchelt was working with an eighty-pound male pit bull at the time. According to the New York Daily News, Febbraio asked whether the dog was "okay," and Borchelt assured him it was. But as Febbraio took a few steps, the dog broke free of the leash and bit him in the groin, removing the end of his penis. As you might imagine, a lawsuit ensued. After a two-day trial, the jury ruled in favor of Febbraio. Borchelt lost to the tune of one million dollars.

Here is a less dramatic incident experienced by a trainer at an initial session with a new client in their home. The trainer was working with the couple's adolescent retriever mix. Because "leave it" was to be taught, she had asked the family for one of the child's socks to use as bait. As the family stood in the kitchen chatting about other things, the sock was left dangling over the top of the garbage can. The dog grabbed the sock and swallowed it. Unfortunately, this resulted in the dog needing surgery. Fortunately for the trainer, the family did not blame her and there were no legal repurcussions.

Training dogs, even when no serious behavior issues are involved, always carries the risk of legal liability. No matter how experienced or accomplished a trainer you are, "stuff happens." The previous stories illustrate just two of the ways accidents can occur, and how easily a trainer could be sued. You might be working on city streets, the dog's collar snaps, and the dog runs into the street. Or a dog becomes ill during your training session, and the client blames it on something you did or on the treats you used. The risk of liability increases exponentially when you work with aggressive dogs. A serious bite may result in litigation, and there is obviously a greater chance of severe injuries when you are working with a dog who is known to be aggressive toward other dogs or people. There are two things you absolutely must have in order to protect yourself: insurance, and an iron-clad liability contract.

Insurance

Just as you wouldn't operate a motor vehicle without proper insurance, you shouldn't operate your business without it. If you are careful and responsible in your training practices, the likelihood is that you will never be sued. However, just as you would not want to be in the position of having to personally pay the other party's damages if you were involved in a car accident, you must take steps to ensure that you will never be in the position of having to pay for injury to another dog or person. (Fortunately for the aforementioned Dr. Borchelt, he had insurance.)

Most companies that offer insurance to dog trainers have a million dollar general liability policy. You might think such a policy would be prohibitively expensive, but it's not. A few hundred dollars per year is average, and it is money well spent. Some companies charge a flat fee, while others have adjustable rates based on annual income. Employees or subcontractors can also be covered under your policy. If you teach group classes, the facility can be added on to your contract as co-insured (most city and county organizations, such as parks and recreation departments, will require this stipulation). These contract riders normally involve a small fee. Be sure to check any prospective contract for payment per occurrence, personal injury limit (that's injury to the client, not to you), and other specifics. Two companies that offer insurance specifically designed for dog trainers are listed in the *Resources* section.

Guarantees

Before we resume focusing on what you'll need, let's take a moment to discuss one thing you most definitely do *not* need: a guarantee. A guarantee should not be offered verbally over the phone, in any type of written materials, or for that matter, at all. It's not that you are unsure of your ability to do the job; it's that you are not fixing a sink! If you were a plumber, you could certainly guarantee your work. However, dog trainers are dealing with living beings, and two of them at that—the dog and the owner. You could be the world's most accomplished trainer, but if the owner does not follow through with your suggestions and practice with the dog, your efforts will have been for naught. The dog, not being an inanimate object, might also act in a way that is unexpected. You cannot "guarantee" that a dog will never again lunge at another dog, any more than you can guarantee that a puppy will never again soil the carpet.

When callers ask whether my company guarantees results, I answer with something along the lines of, "No, we don't. We are highly experienced professionals who have many years of experience and success with the type of issue your dog has. But we do not offer a guarantee because we cannot guarantee *your* behavior." (I soften that last part with a laugh.) "There is no way for us to know that owners will follow through with our suggestions and protocols," I continue, "and if they don't, the dog's behavior may not improve. Besides, dogs are living beings, so no one can guarantee their behavior one hundred percent." The vast majority of callers understand and are accepting of this explanation.

Liability Contract

I would no more conduct a training session without a liability contract than I would conduct one without clothing. I suggest you adopt the same policy. Asking clients to sign a contract takes very little time out of your session (you could even email, fax, or mail the contract in advance), and could potentially save you a lot of time, money, and aggravation. Again, just as with insurance, if you are conducting yourself in a professional manner, liability will probably never be an issue, but it's best to protect yourself just in case.

A well-constructed contract protects both you and those who act as your employees or agents. Having a signed contract does not guarantee that a client will not sue you, but if the agreement is well written, chances are you will not be held liable unless harm has come to the owner or dog as a direct result of an irresponsible action on your part.

The contract should state the date services commence, fees, where the training will take place, and to what services the client is entitled. For example, your contract might stipulate that the client is paying $200 for a package of three in-home sessions for behavior modification. (If you offer packages, I suggest that you also include a stipulation as to the time frame in which the sessions must be completed, or you risk having clients redeem their remaining sessions months later.) With regard to fees, it is perfectly reasonable to charge more for aggression cases than you would for normal training sessions: you will be investing more time and effort, and spending more time on the initial phone call, the history-taking process, and post-session notes. And last but certainly not least, there is more risk to your personal safety.

The contract should have a clause that stipulates that the client assumes the risk if the dog bites another dog or person or causes property damage, both during and after the term of your agreement. The words "and after" are important. Otherwise, theoretically, you could be held liable if the dog bites someone weeks or months after your training services have concluded.

> Another way to protect yourself is to run your business as a Limited Liability Corporation (LLC) or other type of corporation, rather than a sole proprietorship. If you are sued, while your business assets might become involved, your personal ones will not. Discuss with a tax attorney whether incorporating would be beneficial in your particular case. Laws and fees vary by state.

It is beyond the scope of this book, and of my own expertise, to give detailed legal advice. I can, however, point you in the right direction. "Avoiding Liability" is an excellent DVD (see *Resources*) featuring attorney Kenneth Phillips, famous for his work on dog bite cases. Filmed at a seminar, the presentation covers specific wording and clauses that should be included in a dog trainer's liability contract, whether that trainer does in-home or in-kennel training. It also includes liability information for those who place dogs through shelter or rescue groups. Kenneth Phillips' website, Dog Bite Law (www.dogbitelaw.com) is an excellent resource for owners, bite victims, trainers and others. It features dog bite laws for all states, statistics, news stories, and other useful information.

> Be sure to get your contracts printed with carbon copies attached so that you can give clients a copy and keep the original for yourself.

On the following pages you will find a copy of my own liabiity contract. You can also find computer-friendly, ready-to-use liability contracts for private lessons, group classes, and board-and-train arrangements on my CD-ROM "The Dog Trainer's Business Kit." (See *Resources*.) Always have contracts reviewed by an attorney, as laws vary from state to state and particular clauses might not apply in your area. Yes, attorneys can be costly, but so can lawsuits. Besides, the peace of mind is worth it.

Dog Training Services Agreement

This Agreement between _____
(hereinafter referred to as "Client") and _____
acting as agent for Gentle Guidance Dog Training (hereinafter known as "Trainer") pertains to the following:

Dog's name: Breed:
(hereinafter referred to as "Dog")

For good and valuable consideration, the parties agree as follows:

Training Fees:

a.   Client agrees to pay Trainer a nonrefundable fee in the amount of $ _____ for first session and $_____ for each follow-up session. OR

b.   Client agrees to pay Trainer a nonrefundable fee in the amount of $_____ for a package of _____ sessions, to be paid at first session.

All sessions must be completed within _____ from the date of commencement of contract.

Trainer agrees to provide private lessons for Client and Dog on a lesson-by-lesson basis, the goal being to teach Client how to obedience train and work with Dog. These lessons will take place at Client's home. Trainer will make every reasonable effort to help Client achieve training and behavior modification goals but makes no guarantee of Dog's performance or behavior as a result of providing professional animal behavior consultation. Client understands that he/she and members of the household must follow Trainer's instructions without modification, work with dog daily as recommended, and constantly reinforce the training being given to Dog.

If Dog causes property damage, or bites or injures any dog, animal or person (including but not limited to Trainer and her agents), during or after the term of this Agreement, then Client agrees to pay all resulting losses and damages suffered or incurred by Trainer and her agents, and to defend and indemnify Trainer and her agents from any resulting claims, demands, lawsuits, losses, costs or expenses, including attorney fees. If Dog is injured in a fight or in any other manner during or after the term of the Agreement, Client assumes the risk and agrees that Trainer should not be held responsible for any resulting injuries, losses, damages, costs or expenses.

At Trainer's sole election, Trainer's duties hereunder shall terminate if (a) in Trainer's sole judgment Dog is dangerous or vicious to Trainer or any other person or animal, or interferes with the training of other dogs, or (b) Client breaches any term or condition of this Agreement. Upon termination in accordance with the foregoing, Trainer's duties shall terminate but all other provisions of this Agreement shall continue in full force and effect.

This Agreement is binding upon Client, spouse of Client, and children of Client. This Agreement supersedes all prior discussions, representations, warranties and agreements of the parties, and expresses the entire agreement between Client and Trainer regarding the matters described above. The parties confirm that, except for that which is specifically written in this Agreement, no promises, representations or oral understandings have been made with regard to Dog or anything else. Without limiting the generality of the foregoing, Client acknowledges that Trainer has not represented, promised, guaranteed or warranted that Dog will never bite, that Dog will not be dangerous or vicious in the future, that Dog will not exhibit other behavioral problems, or that the results of training will last for any particular amount of time. This Agreement may be amended only by a written instrument signed by both Client and Trainer. Any remedy provided in this Agreement is in addition to any and all other remedies provided by law or equity. If any provision of this Agreement is invalid, void or unenforceable, they will be severed and the remaining provisions shall be given full force and effect.

Executed on this _____ day of _____, 2_____.

Trainer: Client:

_____   _____

_____   _____
        (print name)   (print name)

Part II

Pre-Session
Considerations

Phone Screening

It all begins with a phone call. The way you handle that initial inquiry about your services can not only turn a caller into a client, but can supply vital information about an aggressive dog—so long as you ask the right questions in the right way. While the phone conversation is not meant to be a complete history-taking event, the information you glean will be crucial to determining whether you want to take the case. And if the dog is aggressive toward people, the details you collect will allow you to arrange the environment so as to ensure your safety upon entering the home, and maintain it during the session.

"He's Really Sweet, But…"

You will find that many callers begin by saying something like, "He's a really good dog. He's sweet, he's well trained, and he's so good with our kids.…" Remain quiet and they will go on to supply the "but." Most owners feel the need to preemptively defend their dog, to explain that what they are about to tell you doesn't mean the dog is "bad," but rather, that he acts badly some of the time—which is exactly right. No matter what the caller relates during the conversation, strive to keep your words and vocal tone free of judgment. Let's say Nancy calls and tells you that Gizmo, her normally sweet, playful Jack Russell terrier, bit seven-year-old Stephen on the face. It's one thing to get the details in a compassionate manner, and quite another to imply by your response or tone that there is obviously something wrong with Gizmo, or that Nancy or Stephen are at fault.

Normally, when a trainer is called for help in working with basic obedience skills or manners issues, the owner is on an even emotional keel. There may even be an air of excitement about embarking on this new adventure; at the worst, the caller may be frustrated with the dog's bad habits. But the majority of the time when someone calls for help with an aggression issue, the person is distraught. A developing aggression issue is upsetting enough, but sometimes the trainer is being consulted only after a serious incident has occurred. Families will often tolerate bites to the parents, and even threatening behavior toward the kids, only seeking help after someone outside the family has been bitten. The threat of a lawsuit often makes for a very effective wakeup call.

> Some callers will inform you that if you cannot "fix" the problem, the dog is going to the shelter—which, for an aggressive dog, translates to "will be euthanized." It may be that one member of the family has made this decision and handed down the ultimatum to another, who has now handed it to you. Don't allow yourself to be party to this type of emotional blackmail. Calm the person, get the details, and then agree to help—*if* you feel the case is one you want to handle.

Many callers are not only upset, but feel guilty, as though they have failed their dog. Some even feel that the dog's behavior is somehow their fault. Take care not to make them feel worse. The last thing a caller needs after relating a bite incident involving a child is a trainer asking in what is perceived as an accusing tone, "Where were *you* when this happened?"

In some severe cases, callers already know deep down that the dog's only real options are to be rehomed or euthanized. Those people are seeking a professional opinion to confirm what they already suspect. Be compassionate, be supportive, and keep your tone of voice non-judgmental. Get the information in as professional a manner as possible so that you can be of assistance.

> The "Grain of Salt" Rule: Some owners will either overstate or downplay their dog's problems. Some dogs are not nearly as dangerous as their owners make them out to be, but are merely ill-mannered. On the flip side, I have heard puncture wounds referred to as "nipping." Some owners seem to have forgotten about past bite incidents, while others are in denial about the severity of their dog's issues. Take what owners say with a grain of salt—okay, sometimes a mountain of salt!

What to Ask

Following are some questions to ask during the initial phone conversation. You will explore these questions in more depth at the session, so there is no need to spend extensive time on them on the phone. Twenty minutes should suffice to get this basic information.

What is your main concern?

Callers are often so distressed and/or unfocused that it can be difficult to pinpoint the issue about which they are calling. Encourage them to focus by asking them to define the main problem. Sometimes a caller will begin by describing simple training problems such as pulling on leash or jumping on family members, and then, only toward the end of the conversation, mention an aggression issue almost as an afterthought. In those cases, it is important for you to assure the caller that while the other concerns will be addressed, the aggression issue is the one that requires immediate attention. Explain why. A dog who pulls on leash is most likely not going to hurt anyone; a dog who bites might well end up dead. I would not suggest using those exact words, but the point needs to be made that the aggression issue must be the first priority.

Have there been any incidents of growling, lunging, biting, or any other type of threatening behavior?

This question should be asked in response to a statement that the dog is "aggressive" or some other allusion to the dog's reactive behavior. Some of the questions that follow will be pertinent and some will not, depending on the answer to this question. Ask the ones that apply.

When did the incident occur?

There was probably a specific incident that spurred the call for help. That event is likely to have happened within the last day or two, since owners inevitably feel most desperate right after an aggressive episode has taken place. Of course, there might not have been an actual bite. It could be that the dog is a budding adolescent who has just begun to air snap or growl, and the owner has wisely chosen to address the problem before it worsens. Whatever the case, finding out when the incident occurred, if there was one, will always provide crucial information.

What were the circumstances?

This is where you will have to use your social skills to get a brief synopsis rather than a rambling, in-depth recitation of the incident. That can be a bit challenging, especially if the person is distressed. But it is enough to know for now that the dog had a bone, the child reached for it, and the dog bit the child. Or that the dog was off-leash at the park, another dog approached, and there was a fight. You might want to get a bit more detail, but save the in-depth discussion for the in-person interview. Interrupt gently if you must, summarize the problem, and ask whether your synopsis is accurate.

On what part of the body was the bite?

This is a question that can be answered quickly and will give you a better idea of the severity of the aggression. A case where a dog bit a child on the face may be more serious than one where a dog bit a child's hand. I say *may* be because the rest of the details will help to yield a more complete picture—but for now, this is useful, bare-bones information.

Can you describe the bite? Did the bite break the skin? If so, was it a tear or a puncture?

The information you are seeking here is a description of the intensity and severity of the bite. Was it one bite and release, or were there multiple bite wounds? Did the bite break the skin and if so, was it a tear or a puncture? Was there bruising? Was there blood? Ask for these details in those specific terms, rather than asking whether the bite was "serious" or "severe," as those descriptors are subject to interpretation.

    The severity of the bite may provide a clue as to how long the dog has had the problem. For example, a dog who inflicts multiple puncture wounds is probably a confident dog who has had plenty of practice biting. This is especially useful information if the dog was recently adopted. Since the owners probably have no idea of the dog's previous history, so far as they know, this is the first time the dog has ever bitten. (I have yet to meet an adopter who is aware that their new family member has a bite history.) You will get more detailed information on the bite during the history-taking process, but extracting this much information on the phone can help to determine whether you feel comfortable taking the case.

Why are you seeking help at this time?

There may have been previous threatening or injurious incidents, but something about this particular one has triggered a call for help. It may be that a person outside the family has been bitten, and the owner fears a lawsuit. A passerby's dog may have been injured. Perhaps the child who lives with the dog has been bitten. Or, the person's living arrangements are about to change, and the dog will be required to behave in a non-threatening manner in the new environment. (I have received numerous calls from women who were about to move in with a boyfriend, both parties have dogs, and one of the dogs is dog-aggressive.)

The response to your question may also reveal that someone in the family is threatening to give the dog away or put him down unless something is done. In any case, the answer to this question will give you an idea of how urgent the situation is, how quickly it needs to be resolved, and whether that expectation is realistic.

Have there been other incidents where your dog threatened or bit someone?

Often callers will neglect to mention other incidents unless prompted. In the average dog owner's mind, the fact that the dog growls at their own child on a regular basis when the child corners him or pulls his fur may not be as important as the fact that the dog actually bit the next-door neighbor's child. But these things are crucial for trainers to know.

There is a huge difference in an aggression case that involves a first bite versus one in which the dog has bitten the husband, the child, the neighbor, and the gardener. If the dog has bitten others, you will gather detailed information about each of the incidents at the session. For now, the response is enough to give you a clue to the complexity of the issue.

Do you have children? If so, what are their ages?

Depending on the type of aggression, whether there are children in the home can be a determining factor in the gravity of the case. It is possible that the dog has bitten the child, but there are also less obvious scenarios that can involve children. For example, if two dogs are fighting in the home, a child could easily be injured when a fight breaks out. If a dog guards resources, the situation is more potentially dangerous if there are children who crawl on the floor, or kids who might attempt to take something from the dog or drop something and then grab for it at the same time as the dog does.

When implementing a management plan, older children can often be depended on to keep gates locked and doors closed, and to act in an appropriate manner around the dog in specific circumstances—for example, to leave the dog alone when he's eating or has a bone. But if the dog is to stay in a home with younger children, the program must involve strict parental supervision and management.

What is your goal for your dog?

You might be thinking that the obvious answer would be, "We'd like him to stop biting people!" But it's not that simple. Take, for example, a dog who is aggressive toward unfamiliar dogs. The owner's goal might be, "We want him to be able to play with other dogs off-leash," which may or may not be possible, or, "We want to be able to walk him down the street without him lunging at other dogs," which should be possible in most cases. It is important that you establish the caller's goals so you can decide whether they are realistic and in the realm of your capabilities.

What does your dog do when an unfamiliar adult visitor enters your home?

Notice that the question is phrased "What does your dog do?" rather than the more general "How is your dog with visitors?" The latter is open to interpretation. One person's idea of a dog being "fine" is another person's idea of a dog acting aggressively. You need to ferret out exactly what the dog *does*. That might be easier said than done, as many owners are not accustomed to giving the type of neutral observational description that trainers seek. If the person exclaims, "He goes crazy!" your job is to ask the person to define "goes crazy." If the caller says the dog "is sort of friendly," ask what the dog physically *does*. If you must, ask specifically whether the dog barks, growls, or moves toward the person or away.

Keep prodding for details until you have a realistic idea of what to expect—and even then, stay safe by not taking the person's word as one-hundred percent accurate until you have seen the behavior yourself!

When was the last time you had a visitor who is unfamiliar to your dog?

If you ask the previous question but neglect this one, you chance encountering a dog who was acting perfectly friendly toward strangers at the age of, say, five months, but is now ten months old and the owners are unaware that he is becoming an aggressive adolescent. If the person is calling because the dog lunges at people on walks, but she hasn't had visitors in the last few months, she might not realize the dog has also become aggressive toward people entering the home. The bottom line is, if the person has not had a visitor recently who is unfamiliar to the dog, assume the dog's behavior toward unfamiliar people is currently unknown.

Be sure to ask the last two questions even if it does not seem as though the dog would pose any danger to you. In fact, I suggest asking them even for non-aggression-related appointments. Even if only one in a hundred queries yields the answer, "Well…to tell the truth, I'm not sure how he'd be with someone new nowadays" or, "He did try to bite the delivery man last week," it's worth your having taken the time to ask.

Does your dog have any medical issues?

Because illness and physical maladies can influence behavior, it is important not to neglect this question. The reason to ask it on the phone (as well as to repeat the question at the in-person interview) is that you may want to recommend that the caller see a veterinarian before scheduling an appointment with you.

Medical conditions should be suspected in cases of sudden onset aggression, especially where no aggression has been previously observed. (Note that there is a difference between a year-and-a-half old dog beginning to show aggression—often related to the transition into adulthood—and a five-year-old dog displaying a sudden change in behavior. Either way, a veterinary exam should be done to rule out physical causes.) If you do advise a vet exam, suggest that blood work be done, including a full thyroid panel, and that the vet check for musculoskeletal issues. The vet may suggest other tests as well.

Checklist for Phone Screening

1. What is your main concern?

2. Have there been any incidents of growling, lunging, biting, or any other type of threatening behavior?

3. When did the incident occur?

4. What were the circumstances?

5. On what part of the body was the bite?

6. Can you describe the bite? Did it break the skin? If so, was it a tear or a puncture?

7. Why are you seeking help at this time?

8. Have there been other incidents where your dog threatened or bit someone?

9. Do you have children? If so, what are their ages?

10. What is your goal for your dog?

11. What does your dog do when an unfamiliar adult visitor enters your home?

12. When was the last time you had a visitor who is unfamiliar to your dog?

13. Does your dog have any medical issues?

Other Phone Considerations

Unrealistic Expectations

When a potential client calls about an aggression issue, it is important that you offer a realistic idea of what is and is not possible. For example, you might advise the owner of a dog who is aggressive on walks that getting the dog to walk nicely past other dogs on leash is an achievable goal. You might tell another caller that you have had success treating resource guarding issues such as the one being described. But if someone has an unrealistic expectation, it is best to set things straight before deciding whether to set an appointment.

Consider the following phone dialogue:

"Hi. I'm calling because my shepherd/Rottie mix Brutus has a problem with other dogs. I really need your help."

"We'd be happy to help. When you say Brutus has a problem with other dogs, what do you mean exactly?"

"Well, he lunges at other dogs when we're on walks. And sometimes he gets into fights at the dog park. Last week it happened again and the other owner got really angry. I'm worried that we might get into trouble if this keeps happening, or that we'll get kicked out of the park."

"Do you have a sense of how the fights normally start, and has there been physical damage to either dog?"

"Oh, I know how they start. Brutus either likes another dog or he doesn't. And if he doesn't, there'll be a fight. He just goes after the dog. And yes, he's sent two of the dogs to the vet, but I paid the bills, so it was okay."

"How old is Brutus, and how many times has he been in fights?"

"He's five years old. There's been five, maybe six fights now, all at the park."

"Well, I certainly understand your concern and give you credit for addressing the problem rather than letting it continue. But I need to know, what is your goal for Brutus? Because although we can certainly work with you to help change his behavior, it's possible that Brutus is just not a good candidate for an off-leash area with other dogs."

"Well, I need him to be, because we go to the dog park every night and I take my kids and we all really enjoy it. He has to be okay off-leash at the park."

Based on this brief description of Brutus' issues, it is impossible to predict with certainty whether he could eventually be safe off-leash around other dogs. But based on the history offered, there is a definite possibility that the caller's goal is unrealistic, and it is your job to say so. In this case, you might ask whether the owner would be amenable to your conducting an evaluation, doing a few sessions to get Brutus behaving better on-leash around other dogs, and then helping her to reevaluate her goals. If she agrees, you will get the opportunity to show her over time what is and is not possible. But if a caller is adamant about needing to achieve a goal that you *know* is unrealistic, it is better to refuse the business than to take the case on the pretense that you can help.

~ * ~ * ~ *~ * ~ * ~ *~ * ~ * ~ *~ * ~ * ~ *

A trainer friend received a call from a woman who wanted her twelve-year-old pointer to stop being aggressive toward other dogs. You're probably wondering why the woman was calling at this late stage of the game. As it happened, the family was moving to another part of the country where their back yard was to have an underground electrical fence instead of a solid, chain link fence, and she didn't want her dog to cross the threshold in pursuit of another dog. What are the chances that a twelve-year-old dog who has been dog-aggressive for most of his life is going to completely stop being so? Very slim.

We trainers "teach old dogs new tricks" all the time. But teaching something new is very different than modifying a behavior that has become habitual over many years. It's the difference between your learning a few words in a new language, and changing a long-established habit such as brushing your teeth with your right hand. The family of the pointer can certainly expect to see some improvement, and it is even possible that the dog can be trained not to run after other dogs when in the yard. But realistically, that dog is not likely to be socializing with other dogs any time soon.

Sometimes the problem is not so much how long the behavior has been going on, but the intensity of it. Just the other day, a trainer friend told me about a client he'd gone to see. The dog had literally bitten the owner's lip off. The family loved the dog, and despite her injuries, the owner wanted to know what they could do to keep the dog. And she had kids under the age of three. As you might suspect, he advised her that the situation was not workable.

The Instant Fix

Most pet owners have no idea of how much time and effort goes into modifying the behavior of a dog who is acting aggressively. They may have their own ideas about how fast a specific issue should be resolved; some might even think it will take only one session. An experienced trainer who is using positive, scientifically sound methods should get expedient results, but a serious aggression problem is not likely to be "fixed" in just one meeting.

The longer a dog has been acting aggressively, the longer the behavior is likely to take to change. In most cases it will take longer to modify the behavior of a five-year-old dog who has been attacking other dogs for three years than it would to stop a five-month-old puppy from snapping at strangers. Unless the issue is minor, let the caller know that this is not going to be a one-session fix.

Session Overview

Part of giving callers a realistic overview of what to expect from your company's services is letting them know what will take place at the initial session. Due to the complex nature of aggression issues, quite a bit of time will be spent gathering information. Observing the dog, discussing his behavior, pinpointing triggers, and delving into past incidents will provide puzzle pieces that form a picture of the overall issue and how to proceed. This process takes time and should not be rushed. Some clients expect that you are going to walk in the door, grab the dog by the leash, and wrestle him into submission, thereby solving the problem instantly. That is not the way a knowledgeable, experienced professional trainer behaves!

Explain that after taking a thorough history, you will offer an initial evaluation and outline a behavior modification protocol. Explain too that you will most likely be teaching a few skills that should be practiced before the following session. If your caller balks at the idea of working with the dog between sessions, it is time to discuss what will be required in terms of time and effort.

> Although there are some trainers who limit the first session to history-taking only, I recommend teaching a skill or two at the first session, so you can put them to good use at the next one. Teaching skills right away also demonstrates that that you are able to work well with the dog, thereby creating buy-in, which increases the chances that the owner will follow your suggestions.

Gauging Compliance

Without seeing a dog and taking an in-depth history, it is difficult to formulate an educated guess as to how long it might take to modify a particular behavior. While you might not be able to provide exact figures, it is important that callers realize that behavior modification does not happen overnight, and that they will be expected to work with the dog on a daily basis between sessions. In fact, a major factor in the success of any behavior modification program is the skill and consistency of the owner.

For a simple issue such as mild resource guarding, one or two sessions might be all that is needed—but even then the owner may have to continue to practice the exercises now and then. For more severe, well-established aggression issues, it could take weeks or even months to turn the behavior around, and it is crucial that prospective clients understand what type of commitment will be required in terms of time, effort, and money.

The person's response to this information can provide a good gauge of potential compliance. If Sheila says that Bosley has been aggressive toward other dogs for a long time, that she and her husband should have addressed the problem sooner, but they are willing to do whatever it takes—great! It sounds as though Sheila has a realistic understanding of the problem and the determination to see the process through. On the other hand, if Beverly sounds surprised that Izzy's long-standing propensity to bite visitors most likely won't be stopped in one session, take it as a warning sign that she might not be willing to stick with the program. People with an "instant gratification" mentality do not make good clients for serious aggression cases.

With the recent surge in popularity of dog training television shows, some people have gotten the impression that what they see on the screen can realistically be accomplished in thirty or sixty minutes. An hour-long training session should, in their minds, be able to turn a dog-aggressive dog into one who happily romps off-leash with other dogs, perhaps while wearing team jerseys and going out for a beer together afterward. It is important to explain that while these shows can be entertaining, the finished product is not representative of what happens in real time. Having spent time behind the scenes, I can assure you that those seamless training sequences you see are the product of lots of prep work, shoots, reshoots, and creative editing. Turn your clients into informed viewers. Entertainment is one thing; reality is another.

Without having seen the dog, it will be impossible to tell your caller exactly how many sessions will be needed. If you sell packages, you could mention your normal package deal and adjust it later if necessary. If you normally work session by session, unless the dog's issues are very mild, explain that an initial two-session commitment is required. I suggest asking for payment for both sessions at the initial one. If the client is not willing to commit to even two sessions, that tells you immediately that she is not going to follow the behavior modification process through to its successful conclusion. On the other hand, if the caller is willing, you have ensured that you will have the chance to take a thorough history and teach skills at the first session, and put those skills into action during the second.

Ensuring a Safe Arrival

The following story originally appeared in my book *One on One: A Dog Trainer's Guide to Private Training*:

I once did a session with a woman who lived in a condo with her human-aggressive border collie. I had instructed her to have the dog contained when I arrived, and gave a detailed description of what that meant and why it was so important. I had no wish to become Pincushion Number Six. I called when I was on my way to remind her once again to have the dog contained. She assured me that was no problem. As I strolled up the line of condos searching for her address, I noticed a woman standing in the middle of the narrow walkway with a leashed black and white mixed breed dog. When I got within six feet of them the dog lunged at me. Although I jumped back just as the dog sprang, because the dog was on a retractable leash, he was able to bite me on the leg three times in rapid succession before I could move completely out of range. I was wearing thick jeans and the bites were minimal, but I was not a happy camper.

If you haven't guessed by now, the woman at the end of the leash was my client. When I asked what she had been thinking, her answer was, "I wanted you to see what he does." It is one thing for you to set up a safe situation so you can see what the dog does. It is quite another for a client to take matters into her own hands. Do yourself a favor: make it crystal clear that unless you specifically ask, you do not need to see "what the dog does."

You might think that was an isolated incident, but you would be amazed at the number of people who truly believe that you need to see their dog biting another dog or person in order for you to solve the problem. To avoid this unfortunate scenario, give specific instructions as to where the dog should be when you arrive. For people-aggressive dogs, you might want to include the phrase, "I don't need to see what the dog does in order to fix the problem."

If a dog's aggression issue is directed toward other dogs but he is perfectly friendly with people, theoretically there is no need to have him contained when you arrive. But having the dog contained when you first walk in, even if the person lets the dog in soon afterward, is useful for a few reasons: it makes for less distractions during the initial few minutes of conversation, keeps the dog from bolting out the door, and acts as a preventive measure in case the dog, unbeknownst to the owner, has become aggressive toward visitors.

My first containment choice for those who live in homes with enclosed back yards is to have the dog in the back yard for the trainer's arrival. Note the word "enclosed." Some houses sit in the middle of a fenced lot, effectively giving the dog free roam of the property. That means when you enter the front gate the dog has full access to *you*, so in addition to asking whether there is a back yard, ask whether it is *fully* enclosed. Many houses have a sliding glass door leading to the back yard, which is another reason I like the dog-outdoors-for-arrival strategy; you can get a good read on the dog's body language and behavior before deciding when to let him in, or whether to let him in at all. Of course, in most cases you will eventually let the dog in, as it would be difficult to work with a dog at a distance through glass unless you're an accomplished magician (in which case you don't need this book, so please put it down immediately and go conjure up some world peace).

I don't mean to give the impression that you should be afraid of the dogs you work with, but a little caution goes a long way. If you work with aggression cases long enough, there will come a time when you thank your lucky stars that you asked to have the dog placed outside for your arrival.

In all the years I have been training, there have only been two dogs I did not feel safe letting in the house. One was furiously hurling himself against the sliding glass door, while literally foaming at the mouth. He had already twice caused the owners injuries that required stitches. There was no doubt that he would have been happy to show off his technique had I let him in. In the second case, the dog was very, very still and very,

very unsettling. The hairs on the back of my neck stood on end just looking at him. (Rigid, focused, locked-and-loaded, ready-to-launch dogs can be a lot more threatening than barky, animated, reactive ones.) This was not a dog who had yet caused harm to a visitor, but I did not want to be the first.

Perhaps you are curious as to what happened with those two dogs. Did I tell the clients, "Sorry, but there's not enough money in the world to deal with *that* dog!" then turn around and leave? No. In the first case I spoke with the woman at length, and it eventually became clear that her husband was the one who had wanted the dog in the first place. She lived in fear of the dog, and for good reason. There were also two children living in the home. Needless to say, my recommendations did not include keeping the dog.

In the case of the second dog, although I did not let him in during that first session, I did work with the client. At the second session, I was able to work hands-on with the dog with good results.

If the person lives in an apartment or does not have a back yard, containment can be accomplished by using a crate or a solid gate—with an emphasis on the word "solid." Not long ago, I went to see a woman who had two English bulldogs. The dogs were actually "Olde English Bulldogges," which are built like tanks. These two weighed sixty-five pounds apiece, and half of the dynamic duo was aggressive toward people. His usual greeting, according to the owner, was to latch on to a visitor's foot and bite down hard, without releasing. Because the woman did not have a fenced yard nor crates, we decided to have the dogs gated indoors for my arrival.

Upon entering the home and closing the door behind me, I saw the dogs off to my right. They were standing in a narrow hallway, across which the client had placed a gate—a plastic gate that would probably do just fine for an average human toddler. But these dogs were more like fur-covered tank babies on steroids! You can probably guess what happened next. As I started to voice my concerns, the dogs worked themselves up into a frenzy of excitement. Within seconds, they had slammed the gate flat and come barreling toward me. The female jumped up on my right side in a friendly greeting attempt, practically knocking me over in the process, while the male latched on to my left foot and, as promised, clamped down hard without releasing.

At this point, I should share that the other reason I'd wanted the dogs behind a gate was because of a back injury that greatly diminished my enjoyment of being jumped on by dogs in any context. When the male latched onto my foot, I calmly bent forward, took hold of his collar, and attempted to pull him away from me. But the contorted position, in combination with my injury, rendered me unable to do so. I calmly asked the client to kindly disengage the dog from my foot and put him elsewhere. After my repeating the request twice she complied, and we carried on with the session. My foot was not damaged, thanks to my having had the forethought to wear sturdy boots. But this is just one story that illustrates the importance of proper containment. My guess is that any trainer who has been in business long enough could supply similar tales.

Dog trainers are accustomed to reacting in a calm, efficient way when dogs do unexpected things like lunge at people. Many members of the general public, however, turn into virtual zombies, frozen, gaping at the scene before them. While that response is understandable, it is not particularly useful in a situation where a dog is behaving in an aggressive manner and the owner's intervention is necessary. One useful tactic, should the owner have "turned zombie," is to call the person's name in a sharp, attention-getting voice. After all, we humans are just as conditioned to respond to our names as are dogs. Once you have the person's attention, give clear, direct instructions in a calm tone, repeating them if necessary.

You might be wondering why I don't recommend simply having owners hold their dog on a leash when you arrive. The reasons have more to do with the two-legged end of the equation than they do the dog. Because most owners are not professional dog handlers, it would be unwise to entrust your safety to them. Owners are also very likely to be nervous, which transmits tension down the leash to the dog. One exception to the no-leashes rule would be when letting the dog in from the yard. If you feel it a necessary safety precaution, have the owner attach a leash or long line to the dog and let the dog drag it so the owner can easily pull him away if necessary.

If no other form of containment is possible, tethering the dog to a heavy piece of furniture far from the door (give explicit instructions on how the collar should be fitted) with a solid leash is acceptable. Plastic-coated steel cable tethers are sturdier and more dependable than leashes, so you might want to bring one along. Have the owner step outside to take the tether from you and return indoors to tether the dog before you enter the home. (See *Resources* for tethers.) Whichever containment method you choose, do not trust your safety to the handling skills of your clients.

Because your appointment might not take place for a week or two after the initial phone inquiry, call the night before to confirm and to remind the person to have the dog properly contained for your arrival. Although you might feel silly doing it, where people-aggressive dogs are concerned, I suggest calling en route to say you are on your way, and to double-check that the dog is contained. Again, there is no reason to expect that most dogs you see will bite you upon arrival, or even during the session; but it is foolish to take unnecessary risks.

Advance Questionnaire

Sending out a questionnaire for your clients to fill out and return in advance of the initial session, whether by mail or email, has many advantages. First and foremost, the responses will offer greater detail about the dog's behavior than the telephone conversation alone. For example, you might have learned during your chat that the dog bit another dog; perhaps you were told where and when the incident occurred, and the extent of the injuries. But the advance questionnaire can turn up other pertinent information such as who was walking the dog that day, whether the dog had been feeling ill, how many incidents had occurred previously, and whether the dog tends to target specific types of dogs. The responses should help to paint a detailed picture of the dog's behavior and incidents to date.

The advance questionnaire also gives family members the opportunity to offer their input, as opposed to your getting only the viewpoint of the person you've spoken with on the phone. Since it might not be possible for all family members to be present at the session, the questionnaire may be your only chance to find out about their experiences and perspectives. As is often discovered at a session, some family members might be totally unaware of the experiences another has had with the dog, or one might have a different perspective about a specific incident.

Client/Dog Relationship

The tone of the responses you get can sometimes offer a glimpse into the psyche of a client and their relationship with the dog. Consider this description of a bite incident:

"When I was walking Buddy, a person with a dog suddenly came around the corner with a dog. Instead of walking nicely past the dog, Buddy

lunged at him. Even though I kept calling his name, Buddy kept trying to pull toward the other dog. He's so strong and stubborn that I couldn't hold him back! He finally bit the other dog. The owner yelled at me and said Buddy has no business being anyone's pet and I'm starting to think maybe she's right. I only hope they don't sue."

That brief statement speaks volumes about the relationship between Buddy and his owner. For one thing, she feels a sense of helplessness in controlling Buddy physically. Whether that is due to a lack of training, inappropriate training equipment, the owner becoming stressed and losing control, or the lack of a strong relationship where Buddy looks to her for direction is something you will learn at the appointment. The description also tells you that Buddy's owner believes he is stubborn. This is a problematic belief, and one that is possibly a filter through which all of Buddy's behavior is being viewed. It is even more troubling that she is beginning to think that Buddy is just not a very good dog.

Now contrast that with this description of this same incident:

"Buddy is normally very good on walks. He doesn't pull on the leash, and if he starts to bark at another dog I can get him under control quickly. Yesterday I was walking him when a person with a dog came around the corner. They appeared so suddenly that they surprised us both! In fact, they were so close that it was too much for Buddy, and he lunged at the dog. Even though I had a good grip on the leash he was able to pull me toward the dog, and Buddy actually bit him. The owner was very upset and I don't blame her. I offered to pay for any vet bills. I know we need to work on teaching me what to do and teaching Buddy better obedience and how not to be so reactive with other dogs."

From the very first sentence, you can tell that although the owner feels badly about the incident, her core belief is that Buddy is a good dog. She understands the gravity of what happened, takes responsibility, and wants to modify Buddy's behavior. More importantly, she believes that his behavior *can* be improved and realizes that part of the solution is teaching *her* what to do. You'll find that quite a bit of pertinent information is discoverable by reading between the lines of the responses you receive.

Compliance

The advance questionnaire can also serve as a preliminary gauge of how compliant the potential client is likely to be. Someone who takes the time to provide all the information requested and to write detailed descriptions is more likely to invest the time and effort to practice with the dog and to follow your suggestions. Although the two contrasting descriptions of the dog bite incident gave very different impressions, each was detailed enough to be useful. Each client obviously spent some time remembering and recording what happened. But now imagine that this description was submitted: "Was walking Buddy. Saw another dog. Buddy bit him." Not all that helpful, is it? While it may be that your client's normal communication style is short and to the point, because the questionnaire specifically asks for as much detail as possible, this might actually be less a "person of few words" than a "person of little effort." These types of responses do not offer enough information and will result in your having to spend that much more time at the session gathering details.

Another way the advance questionnaire demonstrates client compliance is the requirement that it be returned with a non-refundable deposit in advance of the appointment. (Mailing a check is simple enough, and even easier are online payment options such as credit cards and Paypal.) Advance payment makes it much less likely that your clients will cancel, even if the session is scheduled three weeks ahead of time. If they do cancel, at least you will have the deposit, which covers the time you spent on the phone and reading through their responses. I suggest a deposit of approximately one third of the price of your session.

The Questionnaire

Because your goal is to obtain as much information as possible, it is important to include different types of questions: some should ask for specific details, while others should be more general and open-ended. The first type of question will ensure that pertinent information is not omitted, and will guide the client to supply the particulars you are seeking. Examples of specific questions would be "When did the incident occur?" and "Who was present when the incident occurred?"

Open-ended questions, on the other hand, allow the client an opportunity to provide information that you might not have thought to ask for. These types of questions may also give you a better idea of the client's state of mind. "Can you describe the incident?" is an open-ended question.

At minimum, you should request the following information:

- Client's name, address, and contact information
- Dog's breed, age, gender, and whether intact or neutered
- Where the dog was obtained and at what age
- Whether the dog has any medical conditions, injuries, or allergies, is on medication, and when he last received vaccinations
- How long the dog has been in the home
- Other pets in the home
- Percentage of time spent indoors versus outdoors
- What type of food the dog eats and how often he is fed
- What type of exercise is being provided and how often
- What type of equipment is being used on walks
- Level of training, who did the training, and what methods were used
- Where the dog sleeps
- Where the dog is left when no one is home
- Whether the dog is sensitive to sound, touch, or motion
- What the dog's attitude is with unfamiliar dogs
- What the dog's attitude is with unfamiliar people
- How the family would describe the dog's temperament

The form that follows is specifically geared toward aggression issues. You will notice that it is titled "Behavioral Questionnaire" rather than "Aggression Questionnaire." The latter term is more likely to offend some clients, especially those who do not realize the extent of their dog's issues.

When you send this form, attach it to your normal intake form or, if you prefer, combine the two into a specialized form to be used only for aggression cases. If there is more than one person in the family capable of filling out the form, send a copy for each person.

You can find an in-depth advance questionnaire as well as a detailed behavioral questionnaire and other forms on "The Dog Trainer's Business Kit" CD-ROM. (See *Resources*.)

Behavioral Questionnaire

Instructions: Please answer the questions that follow as thoroughly and honestly as possible. If there was a bite or other incident, ask anyone who was present for input. Examples of the type of information that is being sought are included after many of the questions. Once you have completed the questionnaire, please return it with a deposit as discussed.

Does your dog have any medical issues?

Is your dog on medication? If so, which one(s)? For what condition(s), and at what dosage?

When was the last time your dog had a veterinary exam?

When was the last time your dog was vaccinated?

When was the last time your dog had blood work done? What were the results?

Please provide a general description of the issue, including as much description and detail as possible. (Continue on the back of the page if necessary.)

When did this behavior start? *(when he was a puppy; a few months ago)*

Were there any changes in the home environment that corresponded with the change in your dog's behavior? *(my husband has been going on more business trips; we got a new puppy; I injured my foot, so I haven't been able to walk the dog)*

Please provide the following information for the most recent incident, and for each incident that has occurred:

1. When did the incident occur? *(last night; a few weeks ago)*

2. Where did the incident occur? *(kitchen; the couch; on a walk)*

3. Who was present? *(just me; my two-year-old son was with me)*

4. Were other animals present? *(our other dog was there too)*

5. What preceded the incident? *(someone approached his food bowl; a visitor walked in the front door)*

6. Did the dog give any warning signals? *(he growled; he barked; he froze and his body became tense; he stared)*

7. Had the dog been feeling well prior to the incident? *(she'd had an ear infection for the last few days)*

8. If there was a bite:

- What was the location of the bite? *(other dog's ear; my forearm)*

- Did it cause bruising? *(yes; two small bruises an inch apart)*

- Did it break the skin? If so:
  • was it a tear or a puncture wound? Was there blood? *(tear with slight bleeding; puncture wound)*
  • if a puncture wound, how many holes were there?
  • would you describe the wounds as shallow (less than ¼" deep) or deep (¼" deep or more)? *(two very shallow holes)*

- Was there one bite, multiple bites, or a "grab-and-shake"? *(one bite, then he let go; he held on and shook from side to side)*

- Was veterinary or medical attention sought? *(saw a doctor; took the other dog to vet; no)*

9. How did the incident end? *(our dog backed away; I jumped in and pulled the dogs away from each other)*

10. What happened right after the incident? *(I put my dog out in the yard; she lay down and looked contrite; I was angry and hit him)*

11. Was the incident reported to the authorities? Was legal action taken against you? *(the other dog's owner reported it to Animal Control; no and no)*

12. Which of the following best describes your feelings about your dog's behavior issue?

    a. The problem is not that serious, but I am curious about what you would suggest.

    b. The problem is serious and I would like to change it, but if it remains unchanged we will live with it.

    c. The problem is very serious and I would like to change it; if it remains unchanged I will give him/her up or have him/her euthanized.

13. Is there anything else you feel we should know?

Once you have received the completed questionnaire, review it carefully. Highlight any answers you feel are incomplete, comments that signal a need for further inquiry, and any red flags (for example, a response that suggests that the owner might have unrealistic expectations or a distorted view of the dog's behavior). At the session, have the questionnaire on hand as you conduct the interview.

Scheduling

You might think that scheduling an aggression appointment is just like scheduling any other training appointment, determined solely by where a free space appears in your schedule—but there's more to it. In addition to having the available time, there are two major factors you should consider.

Who Should be Present?

It is best to schedule aggression appointments when all family members can be in attendance, with the possible exception of very young children. Information gathering is a vital component of addressing aggression cases and, as previously stated, you will be able to obtain more information and varying points of view with everyone present. Sometimes a child will volunteer information about a situation or incident of which the parents were not even aware. More than once I have listened to a child tell how the dog growled when she tried to take back a toy, and this was the first the parents had heard of it.

Even between adults, communication is sometimes lost in the frantic pace of everyday life. For example, Murphy lunged at another dog on a walk last week, yet in the whirlwind of work, errands, and getting the kids to and from sports practice and other activities, Mom neglected to mention it to Dad.

There is another reason for the whole family to be present: Due to the serious nature of aggression, it is crucial that everyone in the family follow your advice. All family members must be in agreement about management and how to act—or not act—around the dog. We all know that spouses and children tend to take advice more seriously when it comes from a professional than when it comes from a family member. Most kids already understand the concept of "listening to the teacher," so it can be useful for parents to be able to remind them, "Remember what Buddy's teacher said about not going near him while he's eating." If one half of a married couple believes in physically punishing the dog whenever he growls, there is likely to be a much higher compliance rate when the instructions to cease doing so come directly from you, the professional trainer, rather than secondhand from the spouse.

How many times have you returned for a follow-up session for basic obedience and manners only to find that a recommendation you made had been misinterpreted? Perhaps you told the owners to ignore the dog's unwanted jumping, and they somehow generalized that to ignoring him when he demonstrates *any* undesirable behavior, such as chewing on the table leg. Or your instructions were that the puppy be tethered to the couch while the family watches television at night, and if the pup nips, to walk away and ignore him for 30 seconds, then return; but the family is now placing the dog on the tether as a punishment for nipping instead. These types of misunderstandings are infrequent, but they do happen.

It is especially important to prevent misunderstandings and misinterpretations when aggression is involved. The more family members present, the less the likelihood that one person's misunderstanding what you said will cause a problem later on, as the others can help to clear it up. With everyone present at the session, each person can hear your direct, thorough explanations. That greatly lessens the chances of well-meaning spouses or parents thinking they understood what you said, then passing on misinterpreted information, or omitting a crucial point that you made.

If the aggression involves a family member, that person *must* be at the session. If the dog is acting aggressively toward a child, while you will certainly not set up a situation that would put anyone in danger, it would be immensely helpful to have the child present. (Of course, if the dog is so aggressive that he might actually cause someone harm, or the person involved is too afraid to be in the room with the dog, you will conduct the discussion with the dog safely contained elsewhere.)

You may get a vastly different impression from watching the interaction between the child and the dog than you did from the limited information you gathered by phone or on the advance questionnaire. For example, the client had relayed that the dog bit the child while the two were playing on the floor; at the session, however, you notice that the child's idea of play includes kicking the dog. Or the client had said on the phone that the dog bit her daughter "for no reason" when the daughter affectionately hugged him, but you notice that the girl has a "hug" that a professional wrestler would envy.

I don't mean to imply that aggression toward children is always the child's fault. There are plenty of dogs who bite because they are extremely sensitive to motion, and a fast, unexpected movement such as a child running by can trigger an incident; or arousal levels when playing a game such as tug or chase with a child can escalate and boil over into aggression. Even a child unknowingly cornering a fearful dog can result in aggression. Without observing the child interacting with the dog at the session, you might miss a crucial piece of the puzzle.

Videotaping

An excellent habit to cultivate is to ask clients to videotape their dogs acting in the manner that causes concern, in advance of the actual session. Obviously, this does not apply to every type of aggression, and I am certainly not recommending that you encourage clients to set up situations where dogs will fight or bite. Explain carefully that you do not want to put anyone in harm's way for the sake of a few minutes of film footage!

Examples of situations in which videotape would be helpful would be: incidents between two dogs in the home, where play often escalates into mild aggression; the dog tends to lunge and bark at other dogs on walks; or the dog growls and barks if someone enters the house, but will not lunge or snap. In other words, if the aggression tends to happen frequently in everyday situations, and can be managed so as not to lead to an actual bite, it's a good candidate for videotaping. Eliciting the behavior is not being advised; rather, an everyday occurrence is being captured on tape so you can review it at the session.

There are a few good reasons to encourage clients to videotape. It will, of course, give you a clearer picture of what is actually taking place, rather than relying on the client's description. But you might also catch something subtle that the person was not even aware of, such as her own body language when interacting with the dog. The ability to repeat the footage and to play it in slow motion also makes it easier to catch the nuances of the dog's behavior and to point them out to your clients.

Another reason to have your clients videotape the behavior is that dogs have a funny way of morphing from problem children into perfect angels at the mere sight of a trainer. I have been in homes where clients had complained that the dog runs off with the kids' toys or pretty much anything left on the floor. So I taught "leave it," and then tried to apply it using the objects the dog would normally covet as bait. The parents brought out one kid's toy after another, but were unable to get the dog interested in any of them. Can you envision standing in the middle of a room with children's toys and clothing strewn everywhere, with the dog sitting in the middle, not moving a muscle, all but innocently proclaiming, *Who, moi?* Because your presence changes the dynamic, dogs will also act differently toward family members and other pets in the home when you are there. A bonus benefit of videotaping is that you will have the footage to share, should you decide to consult with another trainer. Try to get pre-session videotape whenever possible.

An initial session for an aggression case normally lasts at least ninety minutes, due to the time-consuming nature of the history-taking process. Some trainers prefer to allot two hours. You will get a feel for what works best as you go along, but allow at least ninety minutes so that you are not rushed.

The Sobering Story of Julie

When conducting any type of training session, you should be feeling your best: mentally alert, physically strong, and well rested. Those things become *crucial* when working with aggression issues. It's one thing to misjudge when to fade the food treats on a down-stay, and quite another to misjudge an aggressive dog's body language and intent. You shouldn't be offering evaluations or making decisions that could mean life or death for a dog—or potential injury to you—when you are not at your absolute best.

The experience of a trainer named Julie serves as a sobering example:

Julie had scheduled an appointment with a new client who had a Doberman named Rusty. As Julie had grown up with a sweet, beautiful red Dobie and loved the breed, she was especially looking forward to the session. Unfortunately, when the date arrived, Julie was recovering from the flu. She was still taking antihistamines, was physically exhausted, and felt mentally cloudy. Because the client, Margaret, was extremely distraught over Rusty's recent behavior and had begged for a session as soon as possible, Julie disregarded her physical discomfort and kept the appointment.

Julie is an experienced trainer who normally shows excellent judgment when assessing and treating aggressive dogs. On this particular day, however, she arrived at Margaret's home in a post-flu haze. Rusty's main issue involved aggression toward unfamiliar dogs, and he'd already inflicted serious bites on two dogs by the time he was three years old. Julie's standard operating procedure was to use a basket muzzle when working in public with dog-aggressive dogs. In her unfocused state, she'd neglected to pack the basket muzzle, so she used the only other one on hand—a nylon muzzle.

During the session, Julie and Margaret worked with Rusty on leash around the neighborhood. At one point, Rusty became aroused and tried to lunge at another dog who appeared unexpectedly. Other than that incident, the training went well. By the end of the session, the weather had turned hot. Rusty's breathing became labored. Standing in front of Margaret's house, Julie removed the muzzle. She then bent forward to give Rusty the hand signal to lie down. At that moment, Rusty spied another dog across the street. Without warning, he jumped up and sank his teeth into Julie's breast. He then bit her stomach and arm in rapid succession.

Although Julie would normally have had the strength to hold Rusty away from her by the leash, that day she did not. Margaret attempted to jump between the two of them. Rusty knocked his petite owner to the ground and sank his teeth into her arm. Julie immediately grabbed Rusty by the waist and tried to pull him off Margaret. Rusty swung around and bit Julie again on the stomach. Julie once again tried to hold him away from her, at which point Rusty suddenly lay down and acted for all the world as though nothing out of the ordinary had happened. In fact, he looked as though he wanted to go to sleep.

Now, Julie's was an extreme case, and an odd one at that. It turned out that Rusty had been previously "trained" by another trainer who used very harsh methods, including hanging (choke chain, four paws off the ground) and helicoptering (swinging by a choke chain)—in other words, cruelty, not training. Rusty now had some issues about movement in close proximity to his face while he was on leash, which Margaret hadn't mentioned.

Rusty obviously also had a medical condition; lying down to take a nap immediately after attacking is not normal behavior. Even so, had Julie not been so physically and mentally depleted, the entire episode could have been avoided. First, she would have had a basket muzzle on hand, so it would not have had to have been removed when the weather turned hot. Secondly, she would not have removed the muzzle until after everyone was safely in the house. Last but certainly not least, if Rusty had tried to attack her, she would have had the physical strength to hold him off, and Margaret would not have had to get involved. Julie learned a valuable lesson that day, at a high cost.

No one wants to wait two weeks for an appointment after an aggression incident has occurred. If you can find room in your schedule to accommodate the caller within the next few days, great. But no matter how badly someone begs for immediate assistance, if you are not physically up to it, just say no.

Even when you are in good health, schedule appointments based on your own natural biorhythms. (You'll never see me doing an aggression appointment after 3 p.m., as my brain cells have given up by then and have retired to a comfy couch to watch Oprah and eat chocolate-covered pretzels.) Night owls are wise to schedule aggression appointments in the evenings when they feel most alert, while morning people should see clients early in the day when they are at their best. Of course, between the client's schedule and yours, things won't always work out perfectly, but try to avoid those times of day and those circumstances in which you are less likely to be at the top of your game.

10

What to Wear, What to Bring

What to Wear

When attending a party, deciding what to wear can be a challenge; just ask any woman. With aggression cases, it's easy—your first priority is safety. Although no trainer expects to be bitten at a session, you should be dressed so that if the worst happens, the physical impact is minimized.

If weather permits, a thick, long-sleeved shirt is appropriate and, if cold enough, a jacket as well. Regardless of the climate, wear the most rugged, heavyweight jeans you own. That density of material can be the determining factor between a bruise and a puncture wound. Do not wear any type of clothing that hangs, so as not to encourage grabbing or tugging. (Jewelry that dogs can get tangled in is another no-no.)

Remember the English bulldog who latched on to my foot? Boots are your friend! Make it a habit to wear thick, sturdy boots such as work boots that protect your feet and ankles. Avoid wearing a hat or dark glasses. Hats alter the human silhouette in a way that makes us look strange to dogs, and dark glasses make us look like we have three-inch pupils!

> Some clients will ask you to remove your shoes upon entering the home. While tracking dirt on light carpeting and other cleanliness concerns are understandable, removing footwear puts you at risk. Without shoes, not only can you not get traction, but your feet are exposed to potential damage if the dog bites. Politely explain why removing your shoes will not be possible, and that, if preferable, you can conduct the session outdoors.

Perfume or cologne might be great for a date, but not when that date has four feet and an aggressive disposition. While those scents might seem pleasant to you, dogs have such an incredibly sensitive sense of smell that some find such odors offensive. As a person who is chemically sensitive, I can tell you that certain cleaning products give me headaches and cause me to feel irritable. I can only imagine that a dog would not feel his best when inhaling a strong scent that offends him. Besides, the fact that you smell unusual could cause some dogs to mistrust you—and when working with an aggressive dog, you want that dog to be at his most comfortable and trusting.

What to Bring

Preparation is an important part of any aggression session. A bit of advance planning will reduce the chances of your forgetting to bring along a vital piece of equipment or paperwork. Preparedness requires that in addition to the usual paperwork, handouts, treats, and whatever else you would normally take to a training session, you bring the proper tools to protect yourself, both legally and physically. Here's what you'll need:

Training Services/Liability Contract

As discussed in Chapter Five, protecting yourself legally as well as physically is crucial. Regardless of what type of aggression you are dealing with, one thing you absolutely must take along is a training services/ liability contract. This agreement tells the client what services they will be receiving for their investment, and defines the extent of your liability and theirs. Have the client sign the contract at the beginning of the session; it won't do much good to attempt to have them sign it at the end if a bite or other unfortunate incident has occurred. Give the client a copy and keep the original.

Leashes and Collars

Although you might imagine that owners of aggressive dogs would have collars and leashes that are sturdy and appropriate for their dogs, in many cases, they do not. I have arrived at homes where large, strong, dog-aggressive dogs were being walked on flimsy retractable leashes, and the owners didn't own any other type. I have seen people-aggressive dogs wearing collars that were so frayed that it was a wonder the dog hadn't torn the collar off in a spectacular lunge toward some unfortunate stranger. Keep collars on hand in a variety of sizes. They should be made of sturdy material and have metal buckles. Never depend on plastic, easy-clip closures; they tend to allow the collar to slip and resize, and may break at a crucial moment. Leashes should be made of strong nylon, leather, or other sturdy material, and have a solid metal keychain-style clasp.

Head Halters

Over the last few years, I have come to prefer some of the newer equipment for walking dogs, such as the front-clip body harness. But when working with a dog who might become reactive in public, a head halter wins hands-down.

Head halters allow for better physical control, as the design does not allow dogs to pull with the amount of force they would otherwise be able to generate. A head halter also allows the owner to direct the dog's head if necessary. That ability can be useful if, for example, the aggression sequence toward other dogs typically begins with a hard stare, and the owner is having difficulty getting the dog's attention.

These halters also afford the ability to close the dog's mouth if necessary—handy if the dog is barking or trying to bite—by pulling up gently on the leash. Because of the way head halters are designed, there is no pressure on the dog's neck should the dog attempt to lunge away from or drag the owner. (Short leashes are used with head halters to prevent the dog from running or lunging and then hitting the end of the leash, thereby possibly injuring his neck.)

Although various brands and styles of head halters are available, for reactive dogs, I prefer the Gentle Leader®. The design consists of a soft nylon nose loop that sits at the base of the dog's muzzle, and two straps that connect behind the ears. A plastic clip secures the nose loop, ensuring that it will not slip off. The halter must be fitted correctly: the muzzle loop should be able to move freely from just below the eyes to the beginning of the fleshy part of the dog's nose, but no further. Owners often want to make the nose loop looser because they feel it will make the dog more comfortable, but the opposite is true. If the loop is too loose, not only can it slip off, but it can cause chafing.

The straps should be fitted high, touching the bottom of the skull, and be tight enough so that one finger will barely fit between the straps and the dog's neck. Be sure the leash clip is sturdy but lightweight. (See *Resources* for Premier's web site, where detailed instructions can be found.)

Normally, you would fit a head halter on a dog yourself. But if there is cause for you to feel unsafe doing so, walk the owner through the process, explaining how to check for the correct fit. (Bringing along a stuffed dog to show how to apply the head halter and get the correct fit can also be useful.) Take the dog for a walk and demonstrate the correct usage, either directly or through verbal instructions if the client is handling the dog.

Show your client how to reward the dog for walking along nicely, and if the dog tries to paw the halter off, how to pull up gently, bringing the head up, releasing the tension the moment the dog stops pawing. Encourage your client to keep moving and to maintain an upbeat attitude. It is also crucial to teach owners never to jerk the leash while the dog is wearing a head halter, and that doing so could cause damage to the dog's neck and/or back. Owners who are in the habit of administering corrections with a choke chain may need extra coaching to remember to keep the leash slack.

Note: For brachycephalic dogs (dogs with very short muzzles, such as pugs), if a Gentle Leader® will not fit, try a Snoot Loop instead (see *Resources*).

Many dogs initially protest wearing a head halter by pawing at the muzzle loop, but most eventually accept it. However, for a small percentage of dogs, head halters are not the right choice. These dogs "shut down" when a head halter is placed on them, becoming immobile and looking completely miserable. These are the dogs I think of as having a "shoot me now" expression. For them, although other equipment will not give as much control of the head, another choice must be made.

*Gentle Leader®
head halter*

One alternative to the head halter is the previously mentioned front-clip body harness. Premier offers the Gentle Leader Easy Walk Harness® (not to be confused with the Gentle Leader® head halter). The simple design makes it easy to place on the dog and to remove, and the location of the ring where the leash attaches—on the front strip across the chest—gently discourages pulling. The leash can be attached to the ring of the regular neck collar as well for added safety.

Another alternative is the traditional martingale collar, which looks much like a normal flat buckle collar, but has an extra loop of nylon attached to the first. If the dog pulls, the extra loop tightens, causing the loop around the dog's neck to constrict, thereby preventing the collar from slipping over the dog's head. The effect is not like that of a metal choke chain—the tightening is limited by the design. These collars are often used for sighthounds and other types of dogs who, because of the shape of the neck and head, are prone to slipping out of their collars.

Tethers

Tethers can be extremely useful when working with certain aggression issues, to anchor a dog in place and to keep everyone safe. The last thing

EasyWalk Harness®

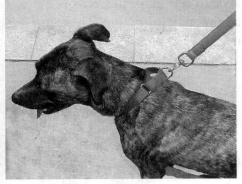

Martingale

you want when practicing a protocol with a dog who guards resources is for the dog to take the offensive and lunge at you or your client. The same applies to handling issues. The tether delineates a safe zone and provides a way to move out of range if necessary. It also allows clients to stay safe when practicing the exercises on their own.

A tether should be four to six feet long, depending on the size of the dog and the specific environment, and made of coated steel cable. Because most stores do not offer these types of tethers in short lengths, having extras on hand to sell to your clients can make things convenient for everyone. (See *Resources* for purchasing information.)

Muzzles

Every trainer who works with aggressive dogs should have muzzles on hand in a variety of sizes and styles. Will you muzzle every potentially aggressive dog you work with? No. But when you are working hands-on with a dog who is a known biter or who may object to being handled in certain ways (nail clipping, for example), a muzzle offers protection. Muzzles can also come in handy when working with dogs who are aggressive toward other dogs in public places.

The benefits of muzzles are many. Not only will having the dog wear a muzzle contribute to your physical safety, but it will contribute to your legal safety as well, since it negates the chance that the dog will bite another dog or person in public. Even in the extremely unlikely circumstance of the dog somehow removing the muzzle (or the muzzle strap breaking) and the dog biting another dog, having used the equipment in the first place shows that you took precautions.

Muzzles also tend to make owners feel more relaxed, and we all know that the owner's state of mind is a crucial factor when working with a stressed-out, reactive dog. Feeling confident that ninety-pound Tonka can't actually hurt another dog even if he lunges toward one will definitely offer his five-foot-one, hundred-pound owner peace of mind.

Muzzles come in two basic types: soft nylon, and basket. Nylon muzzles hold a dog's mouth closed in such a way that, if properly fitted, biting is not possible. Nylon muzzles are useful when working with dogs who may bite when having nails trimmed, being brushed, or being physically handled in any way. Use caution when using nylon muzzles in hot weather; because dogs do not perspire, the ability to open the mouth to pant is necessary. A nylon muzzle should never be used for long periods in hot weather, nor should it be left on an unsupervised dog.

Left:
basket
muzzle

Right:
nylon
muzzle

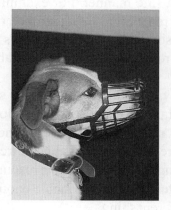 

Basket muzzles are normally made of hard plastic, leather, or metal. They allow the mouth to open wide. Some styles, by virtue of open slats on the sides, allow dogs to accept thinly sliced treats. The ability to offer treats is very useful when working with a classical conditioning program, or to reward a dog for doing the right thing. Basket muzzles are the appropriate choice on hot days, and whenever a dog is going to be wearing the muzzle for more than a very brief period.

Although some scenarios might require that you muzzle a dog on the spur of the moment, it is always best to teach your clients how to acclimate their dogs to the muzzle in advance of them actually having to wear it. For instructions on how to acclimate a dog to a muzzle in a positive, gradual manner, visit online retailer Morrco Pet Supply (see *Resources*). Morrco sells one of my favorite types of muzzle, the Italian plastic basket muzzle, and offers a variety of sizes and styles.

Although muzzles offer some degree of protection, be aware that a dog wearing a basket muzzle can still cause damage. "Muzzle punching"—lunging at and striking a dog or person with the muzzle—can cause bruising and tissue trauma.

Assess-A-Hand®

Created by trainer Sue Sternberg, the Assess-A-Hand® consists of a fake plastic hand on a two-foot wooden dowel, with padding and a shirtsleeve over it. (It is available in a three-foot length as well.) This product is invaluable in that it allows trainers to temperament-test dogs and work with resource guarding issues in a safe manner. For example, a trainer can use the hand to gauge a dog's reaction to being stroked on the back while in possession of a valued resource, or to test the dog's reaction to an attempt to touch or remove that resource. How nice to be able to do all of that from a safe distance!

I had occasion to be extremely grateful to Sue for this skin-saving invention years ago when I temperament-tested a dog for a local shelter. The beautiful black chow hadn't reacted to my interference when in possession of kibble or even progressively more valuable treats such as pig ears. But I had a niggling feeling that the dog was a resource guarder and we just hadn't yet found the item that was valuable enough for him to want to guard. I kept trying different things.

When I finally presented some canned food, allowed the dog to begin eating, then moved the Assess-a-Hand® toward the bowl, he not only bit the plastic hand, but bit it repeatedly, working his way rapidly up the sleeve toward my own hand! It was a pretty spectacular display, but thanks to the combination of the tether and the faux hand, I was not bitten. The Assess-A-Hand® is a tool that, along with tethers and muzzles, should be in every trainer's toolbox. (For purchasing information, see *Resources*.)

SprayShield™ (formerly known as DirectStop™)

If you are working outdoors, you might want to bring along SprayShield™. This pocket-sized product resembles a canister of pepper spray but instead sprays citronella, which most dogs find offensive. It can be sprayed directly into the face of any dog who is posing a threat. There are more preferable approaches to try before resorting to the spray, as described in Chapter Twenty-One, but it is worthwhile to have the product on hand. (Available through pet supply stores and online retailers.)

First Aid Kit

Expect the best, but prepare for the worst: all trainers should keep a first aid kit in their vehicle at all times. The standard items included in any ready-made kit, including antibiotic ointment, hydrogen peroxide, bandages, and gauze, can come in handy in the case of injury to you, your clients, or dogs.

Equipment to Avoid

Since we've discussed equipment to have on hand for working with aggressive dogs, it is only appropriate to mention what *not* to use as well. In short, shock collars (electronic collars or e-collars) have no place in working with aggressive dogs, nor do prong (also called pinch) collars or choke chains.

When working with a dog who is aggressive toward other dogs or strangers, it would be counterproductive to have that dog spy the trigger of his aggression, lunge, then receive a physical correction. That pairing would only cause the dog to associate the unpleasant sensation of the shock, pinch, or sudden constriction around his throat with the trigger, thereby making the problem worse. It's true that the dog might behave while the collar is on, for fear of being corrected—but again, the underlying problem might well become magnified.

11

Two Approaches to Aggression

With all the information available today in books and in the media, a brief discussion of two popular perspectives on dealing with canine aggression is appropriate.

Meeting Aggression with Aggression

Much of the old, traditional style of dog training is based on physical "domination." I know of some old-school trainers who, to this day, begin an aggression session by walking in and immediately rolling the dog to the ground in an attempt to demonstrate who is in charge. (I also know of many owners who have been bitten trying to duplicate this maneuver.)

Other trainers don't do anything quite so dramatic, but their philosophy is centered on the model of dominating and correcting dogs by using physical force, and not letting them "get away with" anything perceived as dominant or aggressive behavior. While strong leadership is an essential cornerstone of addressing aggression issues, the use of physical force is not.

To be fair, I have seen physical force used by trainers on aggressive dogs with the result that the dog stopped acting in the aggressive manner—that is, at that moment, in the presence of the trainer. However, that does not translate to the dog behaving in the same way around the owner. Another problem can arise when one person in the family can physically handle the dog in the coercive way the trainer recommends, but the others cannot. Most people of slight stature and those who have less than the required strength will be less capable of performing techniques that involve the use of physical force. Add to that the fact that, not being a professional, the average owner's timing when administering corrections is not likely to be precise, and you have a recipe for eliciting further aggression and putting people in danger.

Meeting aggression with aggression only addresses the symptoms of the underlying problem, and ultimately creates more aggression. You do not have to be a scientist to understand that the emotions that are associated with aggression—fear, anger, frustration—will not disappear just because a dog is punished for acting on those feelings. In reality, those emotions are simply being suppressed. In all likelihood, they will resurface in other ways and in other situations.

Just as modern, enlightened parents do not beat their children for bad behavior, there is no need to use harsh physical methods such as rough jerking, shaking, shocking, or forcing a dog to the ground. If, for example, a dog lunges at other dogs on walks, jerking or shocking him may make it look as though the problem is magically solved, because it makes the dog stop what he is doing immediately. (Hey, if you smacked me upside the head, I'd stop whatever I was doing at the time too!) But in reality, the punishment only suppresses the dog's behavior, as well as causing fear and frustration. It is also very possible that the dog will associate the pain of the correction with the presence of other dogs, thereby exacerbating the problem. He might even associate the pain with the person who is administering the correction, which can be damaging to the relationship.

Modern Methods

Modern, scientifically-based approaches to behavior modification are kinder and gentler, and entail working with the dog in such a way that the root of the problem is addressed in a safe, gradual manner. Changing the dog's emotional response to other dogs—for example, by pairing tasty treats with the appearance of other dogs, or by giving him an alternate behavior to perform instead of lunging (such as paying attention to the owner)—solves the problem without the attendant fallout associated with the use of harsh physical techniques.

It's not always about using treats, either; if the owner of a dog who has a strong bond with her seemingly disappears every time he lunges at another dog, he learns that being reactive makes his valued resource/ backup disappear. The dog is then more likely to stop lunging at other dogs in the future. (See *Resources* for Tawzer Dog Videos' DVD of Trish King's work with the abandonment technique.) In most cases these methods will not completely modify the dog's behavior in one session, but they are safe, sound methods of treating aggression.

Throughout this book you will find cautions about working with aggressive dogs, as well as important information about how to stay safe. This is not meant to give the impression that you ought to be afraid of the dogs you are working with, although there will be the rare dog you *should* feel frightened of, because the dog is truly dangerous.

While it is wise to take precautions, you ultimately should not be working with aggressive dogs if you are afraid of them. But by researching, practicing, and then carefully applying scientifically sound techniques such as desensitization (gradual exposure to the trigger), counter-conditioning (pairing the trigger with something the dog likes), and operant conditioning (through which you can teach the dog a substitute behavior), you are less likely to trigger an aggressive display. The positive, methodical techniques you use will be easy for your clients to replicate, which ultimately translates to their being able to keep practicing and working successfully with their dogs.

Part III

The
Session

Making an Entrance

So you've scheduled the session for a time of day when you're feeling your best, have read over the completed advance questionnaire, prepared the things you'll need to bring along, and dressed for the occasion. If there is any hint that the dog might be aggressive toward people, you have called ahead to remind the client to have him contained. Now it's time to make your entrance.

If you are absolutely certain from your pre-session information that the dog is friendly with people, there is no need to be concerned about entering the home, other than ensuring that the dog does not dart out the door behind you. If the dog is at all reactive toward strangers he should, per your instructions, be tethered, gated, in the yard, or otherwise contained. But if the dog is at the door because the client neglected to follow directions, use caution. In many cases, a wary dog will make his feelings known by barking, either while backing away (a fear-reactive display), or while alternating lunging toward you with darting away (the dog is conflicted). In fewer cases, the dog will move directly toward you and either give warning signals or actually bite.

Note: It is always a good idea to enter the home carrying a notebook, clipboard, or some other solid item that can be placed between you and the dog if necessary. More on what to do if you are actually bitten in Chapter Twenty.

Reacting to Reactive Behavior

When a dog is displaying conflicted or fear-reactive behavior, your best course of action is *not* to take action: stand perfectly still with your body turned sideways, and your gaze turned downward and to the side. Breathe and keep your body relaxed. This stance does not indicate that you are submitting to the dog in any way, but rather, communicates that you are not a threat. The dog is likely to approach and sniff your pant legs, especially if you smell like other dogs. After allowing for a getting-to-know-you sniff, when you feel it is safe to walk away, keep your movements slow and deliberate. (If you feel that it would not be safe to walk away, ask the client to place the dog on leash and put him elsewhere before you move.)

If an owner has not followed your instructions to have the dog contained, she might open the front door with one hand while holding the dog by the collar with the other. The owner, of course, believes she is simply restraining the dog. But as a trainer, you know that what she is really doing is pumping up the dog's arousal level—dog lunges, gets pulled back, lunges, gets pulled back—which can cause the dog to lunge forward with force when the owner finally lets go. (In fact, this mimics the way dogs are sometimes intentionally agitated for protection work, to get them aroused enough to launch at the nice man in the bite sleeve.) If your client is holding the dog's collar, ask that the dog be put outside or in a contained area for now. The dog's arousal levels will return to normal in the meantime, and then, if and when you feel it is safe, you can let the dog back inside.

> If the client is not busy holding on to the dog's collar, she may want to shake your hand in greeting. Don't do it! While it can be socially awkward to refuse a handshake, the motion of reaching forward can seem threatening to a reactive dog, as can shaking hands over the dog's head. Smile, say hello, and explain why you prefer a verbal greeting.

If the dog is in the yard behind a sliding glass door when you first arrive, you'll have a chance to view his behavior and get a feel for whether it is safe to let him indoors. After giving the dog a few minutes to settle down from the initial excitement of seeing you, if you feel it is safe, allow him to come inside; but as a precaution, have the client attach a leash first. The leash should be left loose to drag on the ground rather than being held. This avoids the client potentially transmitting tension down the leash, and also makes it easy for the person to restrain the dog or for you to hold him off in the event that he unexpectedly lunges or jumps at you.

Bodies in Motion

Non-threatening body language and a calm, even tone of voice will go a long way toward keeping you safe, not only upon making an entrance, but throughout the session. Because some dogs are motion-sensitive, it is best to develop the habit of keeping your movements slow and relaxed, and gestures to a minimum. If you naturally gesture quite a bit when you speak, like I do, you may have to work on that!

Without staring, which could be perceived as a threat, use your peripheral vision to keep an eye on the dog. Take care not to encroach on his personal space, inadvertently corner him, or reach over his head or body. Do not step over the dog at any time. When walking to the table or couch where you will interview the client, do not allow the dog to walk behind you. Many fear-aggressive dogs are butt-biters! Butt-biters are like kids who would never have the courage to confront another child face to face, but instead, run up from behind, smack the kid, then run away. Don't chance it.

Another safety measure involves not being on the dog's physical level. As much as you might love dogs, crouching, bending down, or sitting at the dog's level is unwise when working with a dog who might potentially bite. I know of a trainer who, not long after entering a client's home and greeting the dog, curled up on the floor in a fetal position. I am not sure what her reasoning was, but the dog approached and sniffed her hesitantly. She moved—and he bit her in the face.

Don't take unnecessary chances. If you are uneasy about the dog's temperament, don't even sit on the sofa or at the kitchen table to chat with the client. Remain standing until you feel more secure, and if you do not feel comfortable at all, have the owner put the dog outside.

To Treat or Not to Treat?

Many people, some trainers included, believe that if a dog is offered a treat, he will behave in a friendly manner. In many cases that's true. But when you are dealing with a dog who is nervous around people, and possibly has fear-based aggression issues, whether to offer treats is a judgment call. I wish there were a set of hard and fast rules I could offer to help you determine conclusively whether offering treats to a particular dog would be safe, but the truth is, that kind of judgment comes with experience. In general, if a dog seems threatening or dangerous in any way, or even if you just have an uneasy feeling, you should not attempt to lure him to you with treats.

Some dogs who are conflicted will approach for treats, but once the goodies are gone, all bets are off; the dog may become snappish and possibly dangerous. Sometimes this is due to the dog having a pushy nature and being demanding. But more often it is a matter of the dog having been conflicted about approaching you to begin with, and now that those alluring, wonderful treats are gone, the dog suddenly realizes he is too close for comfort. And we all know what can happen when a dog finds himself at close range in a situation he perceives as dangerous.

This is not meant to give the impression that you should never use treats when working with aggressive dogs. In fact, I use them quite a bit. Just exercise caution when determining how closely you want a particular dog to approach you initially. If you choose to use treats, begin by tossing them (using an underhand motion) to the dog at a distance from you, and then, if you feel comfortable, gradually closer to you. The safest bet, however, is never to offer treats until you have made a solid assessment of a dog's behavior.

13

Taking a History

Obtaining a thorough history is one of the most critical aspects of any aggression case. For that reason, it is crucial that the client be able to give your conversation her undivided attention. If there is a television or radio playing, ask that it be turned off. If there are children who are vying for your client's attention, ask whether there is an activity they could engage in while you chat. If you want the kids' input or need to see them interacting with the dog, call them back in after you've had time to interview the adults alone.

Sit at the kitchen table if possible. Being seated in a hard-backed chair is always safer than being sunk into a plush sofa when the dog is present, and besides, most dogs have good associations with the kitchen.

Leave that Doggy in the Window

In most cases, you will want the dog to be present so you can observe his behavior as you chat with your client. But there are two circumstances under which the dog should be left outside or otherwise contained:

1.
   If the dog poses a potential threat to your safety. In that case, have the owner put him somewhere you can see him as you take the history and vice-versa—outside a sliding glass door leading to the yard is best—so you can assess his behavior and decide whether you feel safe eventually letting him inside. (If your presence causes non-stop barking or other distracting behavior, you will have to place him out of sight.)

2. If the dog's behavior is at the point where rehoming or euthanization may be recommended, leave the dog elsewhere until all vital

information has been gathered. When a dog has bitten another dog or person, the owner may feel angry, guilty, or simply very upset about what the dog has done. The person is likely to have a much more difficult time telling you, "We're wondering if Max will even be able to stay in our home" when sweet, beloved Max is lying at her feet, gazing at her adoringly. Your clients will be better able to relate the facts in a less emotional way without the dog being present. They will also be more likely to give you the complete story without omitting any details that might, in their minds, condemn the dog.

Take Notice

Since in most cases the dog will be present for the history-taking process, here are a few things to note as you speak with the owner:

1. Does the dog seek contact with or attention from the owner? If so, how does the owner respond?

2. How does the dog react if the owner attempts to pet him? Does he welcome the contact, or shy away?

3. Does the dog comply if the owner asks him to do something?

4. What does the owner do if the dog doesn't respond to a request?

5. How does the dog react if the owner asks him to stop doing something, such as seeking attention from one of you?

6. Does the dog avoid or seem afraid of anyone who is present?

These observations will offer clues as to what the family dynamic is like, which is a huge determinant of the success of your behavior modification program. If a bond of love, trust and respect is lacking between the dog and owners, that relationship is the first thing that must be addressed. Owners should be taught how to communicate and interact with the dog, interpret his body language and signals, respond appropriately to his actions, and bond with him through fun activities and reward-based training.

The Art of Interviewing

Along with gathering basic information about the dog's lifestyle, this is the time to delve into the responses from the advance questionnaire. Summarize the response to each question so those present can make comments. Even straightforward answers such as, "Misty has bitten two other dogs" can suddenly become less concrete when there are four people in the room with their own memories and perspectives. When you say, "I see that Misty has bitten two other dogs," the son might pipe up, "She bit a dog on a walk with me, too," yet this is the first the parents have heard of it. It's not uncommon to uncover a lack of family communication during these interviews. Encouraging a collective effort is an excellent way to elicit previously undiscovered information.

In addition to reviewing responses, this is the time to ask for further clarification, paying special attention to any sections you have flagged. For example, "I see that Misty lunged at another dog while Margie was walking her last week. Does Misty often lunge at dogs during walks? Is her behavior any different toward other dogs when Dan walks her? Is she always walked in the same area?" (You are asking that last question because some dogs become territorial if they are walked consistently in the same locale.)

History repeats itself, and so should you. If you feel that you are not getting a complete answer to a particular question, repeat it. I don't mean that you should ask the same question over and over in the same words, prompting your clients to wonder whether you have a short-term memory problem. Rather, phrase the question in a different way, and perhaps even ask it again later in the interview process. You will be amazed at how this simple tactic can spark answers and jog memories.

Reviewing the Advance Questionnaire

Medical Issues

A medical problem can be a crucial piece of the puzzle in some aggression cases. Thyroid imbalance, liver problems, pain, or simply feeling unwell could all contribute to aggressive behavior. If there is any indication that the dog has a medical problem, discuss it thoroughly. Find out how long it has been an issue and what is being done to address it. If the answer indicates something that may be related to the behavior, explain the connection and, if necessary, advise your clients to speak to their veterinarian about further medical tests.

The dog's medical condition prior to a bite incident could play a defining role in your prognosis. It is understandable, and perhaps even excusable, for a dog to bite after surgery when someone pets him too close to the incision site; it is not uncommon for some dogs to display aggressive behavior after being vaccinated; and a dog with a hypothyroid condition can develop swollen, sensitive skin, and bite because it is painful to be touched. But without that information, you might misdiagnose the reasons for the dog's actions. Always take medical causes into account.

Commencement of Behavior

Knowing how long the behavior has been taking place will give you an idea of how long it might take to change. In general, the longer a behavior has been practiced, the longer it is likely to take to respond to attempts at modification. If the issue is a longstanding one, find out why it has not been addressed until now. The answer might be as simple as no one having realized the severity until a serious incident occurred, or that no one really thought it was a big deal—an attitude that should be addressed.

Description of Incidents

Although it can be difficult to remember the details of a traumatic event, especially when things happen as quickly as they do with a dog bite, try to get as many specific details as possible. The answer to question three on the Advance Questionnaire—who was present—can be very telling. For example, if only the wife was present when Misty lunged at a visitor, perhaps Misty only behaves this way when the husband is not at home. It is not uncommon for dogs to see the man of the family as the authority figure, and the wife, less so. Misty may have felt that without a strong leader present, she had to take matters into her own paws. Or perhaps Misty only bites visitors when her housemate Barney the beagle is nearby—a hint that perhaps without Barney's presence, Misty is not as confident.

What preceded the incident can also be very telling. Let's say the dog bit the client's four-year-old daughter. The precursor might have been the child approaching when the dog had a valued chew item; or perhaps the child tried to take a toy back from the dog, who had run off with it. In those cases, you should suspect a resource guarding issue. If the precursor is that the child was simply running across the room, we can infer that the dog has a strong chase drive; whether the bite was a nip (typical of herding breeds) or a serious bite will, along with other factors, help to determine the prognosis. If the precursor to the bite was the child smacking the dog or trying to ride him like a pony, you have an entirely different species in need of behavior modification.

Knowing whether the dog gave any warning signals is very important. *A dog who does not warn before biting is always more dangerous.* Without being forewarned by a signal such as a growl, a person would have little opportunity to back away before a bite is inflicted, and another dog would not have the chance to offer appeasement gestures or to retreat. A lack of warning signals should also alert you that the dog might have been punished for growling in the past, either by current or previous owners. For that reason, the "no warning" response should lead to careful questioning that focuses on whether the dog has been punished for growling and, if so, how. A dog without an intact early warning system is infinitely more challenging and potentially dangerous for a trainer to work with, and more dangerous for the family living with the dog.

> Don't assume that the dog gives no warning signals just because the client says so. Most dog owners are not trained professionals, and subtle canine body language is easy to miss. Even if the dog did growl or give another obvious signal such as an air snap, the person might have been so afraid or upset at the time that the details have been lost to memory.

Bite Description

When it comes to describing the bite, press for as much detail as possible. Knowing where on the body the bite occurred can offer an immediate gauge as to the severity of the situation. Dogs commonly target hands, arms, or legs. Bites often occur on these areas because someone is reaching for something the dog wants, placing an arm or leg between two dogs in an attempt to break up a fight, or the dog's chase drive has been triggered (resulting in bites to the legs). Butt-biting, as previously described, is not uncommon, and is often the product of a fearful canine temperament. A bite to the face, throat, stomach or chest, however, is not only potentially more damaging but may be indicative of a more dangerous dog.

Simply knowing whether a bite caused bruising or broken skin is not enough. A bite might have broken the skin because the dog grabbed someone's arm and the person pulled away, or it could have happened because the dog sank his canines into the person's arm and pulled. In the first example, the bite may have been intended as a warning only, or as something more; in the latter case, the bite was almost surely intended to cause harm.

What the person was wearing at the time may have determined whether the bite caused a bruise or broken skin. The same amount of bite pressure applied to a bare leg will cause more damage than if it were inflicted on a leg encased in thick jeans.

The severity of a bite is vital information, but it does not determine the ultimate prognosis in and of itself. Let's compare the same bite—a single bite and release that leaves two shallow punctures—when administered by two different dogs. The first is a five-year-old dog who has been biting family members for the last two years. The owners have finally called a trainer because the dog bit the neighbor's child. The second is a ten-month-old dog who had three homes before the age of six months and, although not prone to aggressive behavior, never learned proper bite inhibition. While the bite level might be the same, all else being equal, the dog who lacks bite inhibition has a much better prognosis.

Multiple bites normally indicate a more serious problem than a single bite. In most cases, multiple bites demonstrate that the dog was not simply afraid (in which case the likely scenario would be a single-bite-then-retreat), but intended to cause harm.

If the bite victim was someone outside the immediate family, the severity of the bite might be unknown. Often people who are bitten are angry and/or embarrassed, and many do not want to show the wound, especially if it is on a body part that is normally covered by clothing. It is also possible that a bite victim who is angry about the incident could exaggerate the severity of the wound.

As previously discussed, at the extreme end of the bite scale is the grab-and-shake. This should be considered an attack as opposed to a simple bite incident. When a dog holds and shakes another animal, he intends to kill it. Whether the dog has displayed this type of behavior with the family cat, another dog, or a person's arm, the situation is extremely serious and the dog should be considered dangerous. (And yes, we have discussed not labeling dogs, but—let's face it—a dog who mauls a child, for example, is dangerous, period. End of discussion.)

The client's description of how the incident ended and the aftermath can be very telling. The dog might have bitten a passerby, then returned to the owner's side and displayed behavior that most owners would describe as "looking guilty." Or the dog might have been so aroused that the owner had to drag him, still lunging and snarling, away from the person. Those two scenarios paint very different pictures of the dog's state of mind, and may shed light on his motivation.

The aftermath can also tell you something about the owner's state of mind at the time. For example, if the dog bit the child, the owner might have been so angry that she smacked the dog a few times and then threw him out into the yard. Or perhaps the dog bit and released the owner's arm when she went to remove him from the couch; the owner panicked, ran into another room, and called for her husband.

In most cases, the incident will not have been reported to the authorities. Almost universally, bites that are reported do not involve a family member. But regardless of who the dog bit, in many states, victims who seek medical attention at a hospital will be asked for information about the dog, which will then automatically be reported to an animal control agency. Even if a dog bite victim does not need medical attention but reports the incident to animal control, an investigation may be opened. Depending on the dog's history and the severity of the bite, the subsquent investigation could end up calling for the dog to be removed from the home, and eventually to be euthanized.

Owner's Feelings about the Issue

The owner's attitude will inform your entire professional relationship. Working with a client who responds to the question regarding how she feels about the dog's behavior issue (question twelve on the Advance Questionnaire) with the opinion that it is not too serious, will be a completely different experience than working with one who considers it to be a very serious problem. Those two responses also describe very different levels of commitment to the behavior modification process.

Now What?

Once you have finished reviewing the questionnaire and taking a thorough history, ask whether there is anything else the client feels is important for you to know. In my experience, this is traditionally the time when a family member chimes in with some other incident that no one else was aware of, or some bit of information about the dog's behavior that causes you to think *Hmm, I'm sure glad someone mentioned that!*

Summarize the issues and give a brief overview of how you plan to address them. Be sure to explain the commitment of time and effort that will be required, and how long it might take to see results. Do not downplay the latter; very often it can take three weeks or so to see changes in behavior, and it might take months to see major changes in a long-standing issue. *Ask whether the plan sounds feasible.* This is a very important step, and should not be skipped or glossed over. All family members need to be on board, or your efforts may be fruitless.

It is possible that a client will not realistically be able to devote the time necessary to address the dog's issues. Or it may be that the treatment plan you are describing is above and beyond what the person was expecting as far as the amount of effort required. In that case, you should not take the case. Never put yourself in a position where you will be working harder than the client! Explain in a polite and straightforward manner that you understand the lack of time and inability to commit, but under the circumstances, you cannot work with the dog. On the other hand, if all sounds workable, you've got a solid commitment and a great starting point.

Questionnaires

Thanks to the advance questionnaire, you already have some basic information about the dog's issues and lifestyle. (If you did not send out an advance questionnaire, you will need to obtain that information at the session.) Now it's time to get more specific. The questionnaires that follow focus on four common types of aggression: resource guarding, handling issues, aggression toward unfamiliar dogs, and aggression toward visitors. They are meant to serve as guidelines for interviewing your clients, rather than forms for your clients to complete. Although it would be impossible for any form to be truly comprehensive, as any answer could prompt further questioning based on the particular dog and issue, these questions are detailed, specific, and offer an excellent starting point.

Note: Wherever the phrase "your dog" appears, substitute the dog's name. For example, instead of, "How long have you had your dog?" say, "How long have you had Dillon?"

Many of the questions are followed by parenthetical examples of possible answers. These prompts are solely for you and are not meant to be read aloud. It is better to ask the questions in an open-ended manner and allow the client to fill in the blanks. However, if the responses you are receiving are not specific enough, press for details by mentioning some of the items contained in the parentheses.

Resource Guarding

1. How long have you had your dog, and when did the behavior
   first manifest?

2. What items does your dog guard?
   (*food; toys; balls; treats; chew bones; "forbidden" items such as
   socks or shoes; things that are dropped*)

3. Is there a hierarchy to the guarding? In other words, are some items
   more valuable than others, and if so, which ones?
   (*he may guard a toy at times, but if he has a pig ear, watch out!*)

4. Does your dog guard his meals, food bowl, water dish, or
   feeding area?

5. Is the behavior more intense in a specific location?
   (*on the couch; on owner's bed; on dog's bed; in crate;
   under kitchen table*)

6. Does your dog guard items that are not actually in his possession?
   (*food on a countertop; toy at a distance on the floor; a buried bone*)

7. Is there a time of day or other specific circumstance in which
   your dog is more likely to guard?
   (*mostly in the evenings; when he has had less exercise that
   day; when my husband has been off on a business trip; only
   if our other dog is present*)

8. Does your dog guard a specific person or persons from others?
   (*threatens anyone who comes near wife; guards the baby; guards
   child from visitors*)

9. Does your dog guard *from* a specific person or people, or everyone?
   (*growls if the kids come near his food, but not if we do; guards from
   everyone*)

10. Does your dog guard more intensely or frequently from one specific type of person?
    (*man; woman; child*)

11. Does he guard from other dogs, or other pets?
    (*guards bones from our other dog; guards toys from our cat; guards ball at park from other dogs*)

12. What is your dog's reaction if someone approaches when he has a valued possession? Describe the physical display as specifically as possible.
    (*stiffens; freezes; lowers head over item; eats food more quickly; shows whites of the eyes; ears go back; ears move forward; raises hackles; tail raises and stiffens; growls; air snaps*)

13. How closely can someone approach before eliciting a response?
    (*five feet; growling starts upon entering room*)

14. What happens if the person reaches toward the item?
    (*dog hunches over item; growls; air snaps; will attempt to bite hand*)

15. What do family members do when your dog shows this type of reaction?
    (*walk away; take item anyway; reprimand him verbally; use physical action to reprimand*)

16. Has your dog ever been punished for growling or giving warning signs in this or any other situation?
    (*no; yes, he should not be allowed to growl at us*)

17. Would you say the intensity of this behavior has remained at a consistent level, or increased? If more intense, since when? Was there a specific incident or circumstance that preceded or correlated with this increase?
    (*baby becoming a toddler; someone moved out; changed to a food dog finds more valuable; new chew toys; new dog in home*)

18. Has your dog ever bitten a person over a resource? If so, describe each incident including approximate date; specific circumstances; who was present; number of bites; severity of bites; and what occurred right before and after the incident.

19. What, if anything, has been done to address the issue? What were the results?

20. Does your dog have issues about being handled in specific ways, or being picked up or moved? (Handling issues are frequently seen in dogs with resource guarding issues. If handling is an issue as well, see the questionnaire that follows.)

21. Can you offer any other information that might be helpful?

Handling Issues

1. How long have you had your dog and when did the behavior first manifest?

2. How does the behavior manifest?
   (*whips head around and stares; growls; air snaps*)

3. Has your dog ever bitten when someone attempted to handle him? If so, describe what happened. (Full details should include date of incident; who was present; severity of bite; location of bite on body; and what happened before and after the incident.)

4. Are there any specific body parts on which your dog is more sensitive about being handled? (Check whether this correlates with the medical history you have taken.)
   (*top of head; hindquarters; paws*)

5. What specific situations trigger this reaction?
   (*grabbing his collar; picking him up; his feeling unwell that day*)

6. Who does your dog have this reaction with?
   (*one specific family member; all family members; strangers only; everyone*)

7. Does your dog have this reaction when he solicits the petting/handling, or only when a person initiates the interaction?

8. For each of the following, will your dog allow all family members to perform the activity? What about strangers? If he does not allow it, what is his usual reaction?

   - reaching toward him
   - patting the top of his head
   - leaning over him
   - stepping over him
   - picking him up
   - pushing or shoving into him (on couch; in bed)
   - grabbing his collar (to restrain; to pull off furniture)
   - attaching a leash to his collar
   - hugging him
   - restraining him
   - bathing him
   - brushing him
   - checking his ears
   - checking his teeth
   - removing something from his mouth
   - clipping his nails

9. Is your dog less accepting of touch when he is in a specific position?
   (*lying down; on his back*)

10. Is your dog less accepting of touch when he is in a specific location?
    (*on the couch; on your bed; on his bed*)

11. Is your dog less accepting of touch at certain times of day or in specific circumstances?
    (*evenings; upon being awakened*)

12. Is your dog less accepting of touch when he is in possession of food or another valued item?

13. During veterinary visits, do the vet and staff have difficulty handling your dog? Must he be muzzled for exams?

14. At the groomer, does the staff have difficulty handling your dog? Must he be muzzled?

15. Has your dog ever bitten or threatened the veterinary or grooming staff?

16. Has the reactivity to handling remained at a constant level, or become more intense? If more intense, since when? Was there a specific incident that preceded or coincided with this increase?
    (*baby becoming more active; child now having friends visit; someone the dog saw as a leader moving out; dog's arthritis or other physical problem developing or becoming worse; since being put on medication; recent surgery*)

17. Has your dog ever been punished for growling or giving other warning signals in this or any other situation? If so, describe the punishment used.

18. What, if anything, has been done to address the issue? What were the results?

19. Does your dog have any resource guarding issues?
    (These often correlate with handling issues. If so, see the Resource Guarding questionnaire.)

20. Can you offer any other information that might be helpful?

~ * ~ * ~ * ~ * ~ * ~ * ~ * ~ *~ * ~ * ~ * ~ *

Aggression Toward Unfamiliar Dogs

(These questions may be adapted for a dog who displays aggression toward unfamiliar people in public places.)

1. Has your dog been spayed/neutered? (Even though this question was asked during the basic information gathering stage, because it can have a bearing—especially on fighting between male dogs—ask again to be sure.)

2. How long have you had your dog and when did the behavior first manifest?

3. Is your dog sensitive to sound, touch, or movement?

4. At what age was your dog exposed to other dogs? How would you describe his interactions with them at that age?

5. If there are other dogs in the home, how does he get along with them?

6. Does your dog have access to view other dogs passing by your house? (*back yard gate; living room window*)

   If so, how does he respond when a dog passes by?

7. Does your dog fence-fight with neighboring dogs?

8. Are there any dogs that your dog currently plays with or with whom he is comfortable, other than your own dogs? If so, where does this interaction take place?

9. What type of collar and leash are you using to walk your dog?

10. How often is your dog taken for walks, and how long does an average walk last? Do you always follow the same route or walk in the same area?

11. Is your dog always leashed for walks or is he allowed off-leash at times? If so, in what circumstances?
(*allowed off-leash at the park; off-leash on streets*)

If he is allowed off-leash, have you noticed a difference in his behavior toward other dogs off-leash versus leashed? (Note: There are some dogs who are perfectly fine with other dogs while off-leash, but reactive toward them when leashed. This form of reactivity is often termed "leash frustration.")

12. When your dog is taken for a walk, what is his reaction to other dogs? Describe his physical response as specifically as possible.

13. In what percentage of his encounters with other dogs would you say this reaction occurs?

14. Roughly at what distance does this reaction occur?

15. Is your dog's reaction more intense when encountering a specific type of other dog?
(*male; female; unneutered; large; small; prick-eared; stub-tailed; tail curved over back; specific color; specific breed*)

16. Are there any specific actions on the part of unfamiliar dogs that trigger a reaction in your dog?
(*barking; whining; staring; tail wagging; moving toward your dog; running*)

17. Does this reaction occur whether the unfamiliar dog is on the street or behind a fence?

18. Is this reaction displayed only on walks in your own neighborhood, in other specific locations, or everywhere?

19. On walks, when *you* first see another dog on the street, what is your reaction?
(*tense up; tighten the leash; pull your dog to you; talk to your dog*)

20. When your dog reacts to another dog on the street, what is your response?
(*walk him away; make him sit by the side of the road until the other dog passes; use collar to correct him*) (The last example is something I do not recommend, but many people will do.)

How does your dog respond?

21. Is your dog's reaction to other dogs different depending on who is walking him? If so, how?

22. Is your dog ever allowed to greet other dogs on walks? If so:

- does your dog normally approach other dogs, or wait to be approached?
- describe your dog's typical reaction when first meeting another dog
- do you normally tighten the leash for introductions or keep it slack?
- which types of dogs are greetings successful with, if any?
- who is walking your dog when these interactions occur? Is there a difference in your dog's reaction based on who is holding the leash or who is present?

23. Has your dog ever fought with another dog? If so, for each incident, please provide as much detail as possible:

- date of incident
- location
- who was present
- whether dogs were on leash or off
- what breed of dog was involved
- what happened right before incident
- detailed description of incident
- how the fight ended (*the dogs stopped fighting; someone separated them*)
- location of injury on either dog's body
- extent of damage and whether either dog required veterinary care

24. Does your dog ever "warm up" to other dogs with repeated exposures or enough time spent together?

25. If there is another dog in the home, does your dog's reaction to unfamiliar dogs in public differ if the other dog is present? If so, how?

26. Would you say this behavior has remained at a steady level, or become more frequent and/or intense? If more frequent/intense, since when? Was there a specific incident or circumstance that preceded or coincided with this increase?
    (*new dog in neighborhood; walking on new route; different person walking dog; different circumstance in home, such as new baby or longer hours at job; dog's arthritis or other physical problem developing or becoming worse; since being put on medication*)

27. What has been done to address the issue so far? What were the results?

28. Can you offer any other information that might be helpful?

~ * ~ * ~ * ~ * ~ * ~ * ~ * ~ *~ * ~ * ~ * ~ *

Aggression toward Visitors

1. How long have you had your dog and when did the behavior first manifest?

2. Is your dog sensitive to sound, touch, or movement?

3. Does your dog normally have visual access to people passing the house?
   (*window; back yard gate*)

   If so, does he become reactive when a person passes? Describe his physical reaction.
   (*barks; lunges at window; redirects/snaps at nearby person in home*)

4. Where is your dog normally kept when someone comes to the door? (*behind a gate; in the yard; loose in the house*)

5. What is your dog's reaction to the doorbell? What is his reaction to someone knocking?

6. What does your dog do when an unfamiliar person enters the home? (This question should have been answered in detail on the phone as well. Never accept a vague "he's fine" when you are to be the next person in the door!) Describe his physical reaction in as much detail as possible.
    (*barks; lunges; hair stands up on his back; growls; air snaps; runs away*)

    What do you do if your dog has this reaction, and how does he respond?

7. When reacting, does your dog move toward or away from the visitor?

8. When your dog reacts, can you interrupt and get his attention?

9. If your dog is an outdoor dog, how does he react when an unfamiliar person enters the yard? Describe his physical reaction in as much detail as possible. What do you do if your dog has this reaction, and how does he respond? (Additionally, if he is an outdoor dog, one of your first questions after seeing that information on the intake form should be why that is the case.)

10. Whether in the house or yard, with what percentage of visitors does your dog have this reaction?

11. Are there any specific motions or details about the person that tends to trigger this reaction? (*wearing a hat or sunglasses; yelling; gesturing*) Is your dog's reaction stronger with one type of person? (*men; women; children—give age range; elderly; unfamiliar skin color; facial hair; wearing uniform*)

12. Is your dog's reaction to visitors different depending on the time of day? If so, how?

13. Is your dog's reaction to visitors different depending on who is at home? If so, how?

14. If there is another dog in the home, is your dog's reaction to visitors different if that dog is present? If so, how?

15. Does your dog's reaction to an individual visitor lessen with repeated exposures, and/or decrease after the person has been in the home for a period of time? If so, how many exposures and how much time does it normally take?

16. Can visitors eventually pet your dog? Does any specific type of petting elicit a display of fear or aggression?

17. If a visitor stands up, re-enters a room, or walks away, does your dog react? If so, how?

18. Does your dog react if a visitor approaches or interacts with (*hugs; shakes hands with*) a specific family member?

19. Does your dog react if a visitor approaches a specific location (*his dog bed; your bed*) or resource (*bone; food bowl*)?

20. If your dog growls or otherwise warns visitors, what is your reaction, and how does your dog respond to it?

21. Is your dog managed in any way during visits? (*kept on leash; tethered; crated*)

22. Has your dog ever bitten a visitor? If so, for each incident, please describe:

   - date of incident
   - who was present
   - detailed description of incident

- number of bites
- location of bite(s) on body
- severity of bite(s)
- what occurred right before and after the bite(s)

23. Would you say your dog's behavior toward visitors has become more intense or more frequent? If so, did a specific incident or circumstance precede or coincide with this increase?
 (*more people coming to visit; someone moving out or spending less time at home; new baby; dog getting less exercise; dog's arthritis or other physical problem developing or becoming worse; since being put on medication*)

24. What, if anything, has been done to address the issue? What were the results?

25. Can you offer any other information that might be helpful?

Topics to Discuss

Take some time to discuss each of the following topics briefly at the initial session. You will probably find yourself reviewing some of them at follow-up sessions as well.

Normal Canine Behavior

It is important to explain to owners that some canine behavior that humans perceive as aggressive is absolutely normal. Many people expect a dog to never growl, raise his hackles, or even lift the corner of his lip, regardless of the actions of another dog or person. If you were in a grocery store and the man in back of you in line kept jostling you, you would eventually ask him to stop. But if the man were jostling you and you did not have a way to vocalize your displeasure, you might eventually resort to pushing him away. It's the same with dogs. Signals such as growling are a dog's way of saying, "Pardon me, but I'm really not comfortable with what's going on. Kindly back off." Growling and other warning signals do not always indicate an intention to do harm; in fact, they can stop a situation from escalating if the other party heeds the communication.

Teach your clients that dogs may not like every single dog they meet, any more than you like every person you meet. That might seem obvious to you as a trainer, but many people believe their dog should get along with all other dogs, regardless of how obnoxious or poorly mannered the other dogs may be. Sometimes it is perfectly appropriate for a dog to convey to another dog, "That's enough!" Giving your clients a realistic overview of what constitutes normal canine behavior will go a long way toward creating a greater understanding of their own dog's actions and will improve their relationship.

The Development and Modification of Aggression

It is helpful for clients to understand how aggression develops. Most dogs do not go from never having bitten to inflicting multiple puncture wounds on multiple people, without having inflicted progressively more serious bites in between. Aggressive behavior often begins to manifest when a dog enters adolescence, with its accompanying hormonal changes. The dog who was previously fearful slowly gains confidence and may begin to growl, air snap, or bark at the object of his distress in order to increase the distance between them. And it works! Most people and other dogs wisely move away.

As the dog learns that these displays are effective, his ever increasing confidence may lead to biting. Bites normally become progressively harder and more frequent over time (unless the dog never learned bite inhibition, in which case the bites might have more pressure from the start). If your client's dog is an adolescent or young adult, explaining that dogs gain confidence during this stage can help them to understand why their dog is suddenly acting in a manner that seems so foreign. If an adult dog was recently adopted and is inflicting confident, multiple bites, it is important that the owner understand that the dog has almost certainly bitten in the past. Regardless of which stage of development your clients' dogs are in, understanding that aggression tends to worsen over time if left untreated can act as an impetus to comply with and continue the recommended behavior modification plan.

Another aspect of canine behavior that is important for your clients to understand is that even after the behavior modification process is complete, if a dog is not exposed to the trigger of his aggression for a long period of time and then encounters it, the aggression may resurface. You can often change or modify the underlying feeling a dog has toward the object of his reactivity, or help an owner instill an alternate behavior that the dog can perform when the encountering the trigger. With enough time and practice, the behavior should no longer manifest. But is the dog "cured?" No. Hams are "cured." Aggression is not. If the dog is dog-reactive and the owners move to a rural area where he seldom sees other dogs, upon encountering one months later the aggressive behavior may reappear. If a dog is no longer reactive toward the teenage daughter's many visitors, but then she moves out and the house is much quieter, the dog may become reactive to a person who shows up after months of silence.

You may hear the term "rehabilitated" applied to aggressive dogs by some trainers or rescue groups. One trainer was even quoted as saying that "all dogs can be rehabilitated, one hundred percent." That is simply not true, any more than all people who are addicted to drugs or alcohol can be "one hundred percent rehabilitated." We are dealing with living beings. In many cases, we can reduce the manifestation of aggressive behavior through behavior modification programs—that's our job. But, unfortunately, there are dogs who are so dangerous that no responsible, ethical trainer would ever suggest they stay in their homes nor deem them "rehabilitated."

Management and Liability

Management is an important topic to discuss with your clients. Accidents happen when dogs who demonstrate dangerous behavior are not properly managed. Do not assume that your clients understand how to manage their dogs properly in everyday circumstances. You must be specific in your instructions. Proper management means that if a dog is reactive toward strangers who enter the home, he should be crated, placed in the back yard, or otherwise safely contained when visitors are expected. If a dog has displayed aggressive behavior toward other dogs, good management dictates that he not visit the dog park and, in some cases, that he be muzzled for daily walks. If a dog has a resource guarding issue, he should be locked in a crate or other confined area away from children while he eats. It should be stressed to owners that unless they are specifically setting up a situation to address the problem as you have advised, the dog must be managed. Management prevents dogs from practicing unwanted behaviors and keeps everyone safe.

If applicable, liability should also be discussed. Obviously, if the dog is acting in a threatening manner only toward someone in the family, or toward the other family dog, liability is not an issue. But if the dog is reactive toward other dogs and people, the legal ramifications of a bite must be discussed. Let your clients know that if their dog bites another dog or person and a lawsuit results, they could end up losing their home and homeowner's insurance, and the dog could end up being euthanized. That might sound dramatic, but often people do not realize how serious the situation can become if the dog bites. Be compassionate, but don't sugar-coat your statements. Hopefully this direct dialogue will also help to encourage compliance.

Reacting to an Incident

Although you will be working with owners to stop further aggressive incidents, the reality is that "stuff happens." Review with your clients what to do if, despite their best efforts, the dog becomes reactive or actually bites. Many people react to a warning or a bite by yelling or getting physical with the dog. Unfortunately, this can have the effect of increasing the dog's arousal level, thereby causing the behavior to escalate and making the situation even more dangerous. So what *should* your clients do if the dog growls, gives another type of warning, or actually bites them? Defuse the situation as calmly as possible. In most cases, moving away slowly is the safest bet. Keeping the body angled slightly toward the dog while moving away will cut down on the chances of a "butt-bite" and allow the person to monitor the dog. Defusing the situation should not be confused with giving up the leadership role or ignoring the issue. You are advising owners on how to stay safe in a potentially dangerous situation. You will, of course, be helping them to address the underlying problem. Be sure your clients understand that they should call you immediately if there are any incidents.

Many owners believe that punishing their dog for growling will teach the dog to stop being aggressive, when in reality, it only suppresses the dog's way of expressing discomfort. Explain to your clients that although the overall goal is to eliminate the problem so there will be no growling or other disturbing behavior, removing a dog's early warning system is a very bad idea. Punishing a dog for growling can result in a dog who bites with no warning. Having seen many dogs who were already at that stage, I can tell you that I would rather work with a dog who growls any day!

Canine Body Language

It is crucial to discuss canine body language early on, and to point out its nuances as you continue along. While some owners are very tuned in to the subtleties of their dog's silent signals, others are not. Dogs do not normally attack without warning; there is a sequence of events that leads up to a bite. Early signals in the behavior chain may include a stiffening of the body (the tense musculature can often be seen in the face as well), freezing in place, lowered head, curled lip, hard stare, "whale eye" (whites of the eyes showing), piloerection (raised hackles), or a raised, stiffly wagging tail. All of these things can happen within seconds, before a growl is ever issued. Yet the point at which a dog growls or barks is when many people first become aware that there is a potential problem.

As previously mentioned, videotape can be extremely useful when teaching owners to recognize their dog's individual signals. If a dog is reactive toward other dogs on walks, taping and then reviewing it—in slow motion if necessary—can help an owner learn to notice the exact moment the dog begins to react. You should also point out the earliest signs of tension and other significant body language as you and your client work outdoors with the dog together. With practice, the owner will become adept at reading her dog's body language and therefore better at behavior modification. Because the skill does take time to learn, and can feel overwhelming at first to some owners, let your clients know that even if they have not noted a particular signal, but simply feel uneasy about a situation, they should calmly remove the dog from the area.

With certain types of aggression, warning signals may be a bit different. If a dog guards his food bowl, the first sign that he is agitated at someone's approach may be that he begins to eat more quickly, or that he lowers his head over the bowl. A dog who bites when touched on certain areas may attempt to move that part of his body away from the person's hands. Whatever the issue, review with owners the possible warning signals and what to do if they occur.

It is also important that owners be taught to recognize canine stress signals. These include turning away of the head and/or body, averting the gaze, licking the lips, yawning, and even scratching. If a dog licks his lips often during a training session, it could mean that the method of training or even the verbal tone is too intense for his sensitivity level. In a group class, if an owner understands that her dog's yawning or giving another type of stress signal whenever another dog approaches indicates stress, she will be more likely to be watchful about keeping a safe distance from the other dogs.

Human Body Language

In many cases where canine aggression is directed toward a human, the victim has no idea what their body language was communicating to the dog before the bite. For example, the person who "just reached out to pet him on the head" was not aware that many dogs find a palm-down, overhead approach frightening. The mother of the little girl who hugs Fluffy might not recognize that Fluffy's yawning and turning her head away means that she's not comfortable with what she perceives as restraint. Talk about natural behaviors—little girls *love* to hug! Most boys just want to roughhouse (which can be problematic in cases where play arousal boils over into aggression), but for girls, there's nothing better than an I-love-my-puppy cuddle.

Whenever clients tell me their dog loves it when their child hugs him, I ask to see it for myself. While it is true that some dogs do actually enjoy being hugged, and others learn to tolerate it, many dogs truly dislike it; I often see lip-licking or yawning, sometimes in combination with turning away of the head and averting the gaze. It is good practice to point these signals out to your clients so they can learn to recognize them.

It is not only our body language that is perceived by dogs, but our emotional state as well. For example, a leash is not only a tool for walks; it is also a conduit. If the person walking the dog is tense, that tension is transmitted down the leash. When the owner of a dog-aggressive dog takes him for a walk, you can bet that person is vigilantly scanning the environment, on the lookout for potential trouble. She is nervous, and understandably so. When another dog comes into view, the owner's muscles tighten, causing her to tighten up on the leash; that tension signals the dog that there is something to be concerned about. Her very energy field is filled with tension, and the dog senses it. This dynamic of energy transfer is one reason why, when a trainer walks a dog-aggressive dog down the street, there is often much less of a reaction on the dog's part than when the owner walks him. The trainer exudes an air of cool confidence and keeps the leash slack, so the dog feels there is nothing to worry about. While changing the owner's emotional state won't solve the problem all by itself, it can play a vital role.

Neutering

Studies have shown that neutering a male dog can lessen his aggression toward other male dogs.[1] Whether that is because other male dogs no longer see him as a threat or because the decreased testosterone levels change his behavior is the subject of speculation. But educating clients who have intact male dog-aggressive dogs about neutering is crucial. There is also anecdotal evidence that neutering a male dog can lower other types of aggression, such as dominance aggression toward his owners.

It is said that in wolf packs, males fight for rank and females fight to the death. In fights between male dogs, the action is typically accompanied by loud vocalizations—think barroom brawl. This raucous-sounding confrontation is typical, whether or not any actual damage occurs. The female-female style of fighting falls more into the "silent but deadly" category; there is less posturing and vocalization, but serious damage often occurs.

We don't often consider the effect that spaying a female dog may have on aggression. When two female dogs in a home are fighting, especially if they are approximately the same age, the potential exists for severe injury or even death. If the dogs are not spayed and the fights occur during estrus, either the dogs must be separated during those times, or spaying will have to be part of the solution. There have not been many studies on the behavioral effects of spaying bitches, although one study found that females who were already showing signs of aggression and were then spayed at less than twelve months of age showed an apparent *increase* in "aggressive dominance towards owners."[2]

Equipment

Regardless of the type and severity of the aggression, a discussion of proper equipment is mandatory. If a dog displays aggression toward other dogs or people on walks, equipment such as a head halter and a strong, non-retractable leash should be discussed, along with a basket muzzle if necessary. If the aggression is directed toward family members who try to handle the dog in a certain way—for example, clipping his nails—a discussion of how to use a nylon muzzle when practicing behavior modification exercises would be appropriate. A tether would be useful as well. Whether you recommend a nylon muzzle or a basket muzzle, explain how to acclimate the dog to it gradually and instruct the client to practice leaving it on the dog for short, supervised periods before you return for the next session.

Whatever type of equipment you suggest, it is best to have it on hand so that you can fit it correctly and demonstrate how to place in on the dog, use it properly, and remove it safely. If you do not sell a particular type of equipment, give specific recommendations including, whenever possible, where to purchase it. At the following session, be sure the equipment is fitted correctly and review the proper usage.

Nutrition

Nutrition plays a critical role in behavior. Just as eating too much sugar or drinking too much caffeine can make people irritable and hyperactive, poor nutrition can play a major role in a dog's emotional state. Teach clients how to read labels on dry and canned dog foods so they can choose one with quality ingredients. At minimum, they should be feeding a product that lists meat as its first two ingredients, preferably whole meats such as chicken or lamb, rather than meat meal, or even worse, meat by-products. The food should be free of corn, which, through a series of chemical reactions in the body, lowers serotonin levels in the brain. Serotonin is a naturally occurring neurotransmitter that contributes to a feeling of calm—and you want the dog to be as calm as possible. (For an in-depth discussion of the effects of nutrition on canine behavior, see my book *Help for Your Fearful Dog* or James O'Heare's *Canine Neuropsychology* in *Resources*.)

Another facet of feeding that should be discussed is timing. The dog should be eating on a fairly regular schedule rather than the food being available all day. The reason has to do with leadership. Food—that invaluable, life-giving resource—should be coming from the owners rather than from that round thing that's always magically full. Most adult dogs can be fed twice daily (this keeps the dog's blood sugar levels more even than eating one meal per day), with the food removed after ten to fifteen minutes if the dog has not finished. No dog will starve himself, and most dogs adjust to a new feeding schedule fairly easily. Obviously, if the dog is a young puppy and the clients are working all day, the food must be left available for the time being. If the dog has medical issues or is tiny, suggest that your clients discuss any proposed changes with their veterinarian.

> In almost all aggression cases, it is useful to have the owner hand-feed the dog (assuming it is safe to do so) for at least two weeks. Doing so elevates the status of the owner and helps to strengthen the dog-owner bond.

Exercise and Mental Stimulation

Exercise, or lack of it, can have a huge effect on a dog's behavior. Exercise raises serotonin levels in the brains of both dogs and people. Just as people feel more relaxed after a long jog or a workout at the gym, dogs are calmer when given regular exercise. That exercise may be supplied in the form of daily walks, hiking, playing with other dogs, swimming, or dog sports such as agility. Of course, some forms of exercise will be off-limits if the dog is aggressive with other dogs or with people.

Mental stimulation also plays a vital role in contributing to a dog's calm state of mind. Chew toys that require dogs to figure out how to get at the goodies inside, training exercises, and even trick training are all great ways to keep a dog's mind engaged. The more mental stimulation and physical exercise a dog gets, the less excess energy is available to be funneled into aggressive behavior. The old saying "a tired dog is a good dog" is especially applicable when that dog has aggressive tendencies.

Leadership – Or, "The Clint Eastwood Effect"

It is crucial for a dog with aggression issues to have a strong human leader. The majority of canine aggression issues are fear-based, and an anxious dog will feel much more at ease if he knows his owner will keep him safe in the face of a threat. Imagine that you are visiting a foreign country where your tour guide is new to the job, doesn't speak the local language very well, and seems unsure of himself. Now imagine that as you are walking down a crowded street, a riot breaks out. Will you look to your tour guide for direction? Not likely; instead, you'd probably take matters into your own hands and run for safety. Now let's imagine that Clint Eastwood is your tour guide. He's experienced, knowledgeable, and exudes an air of confidence. In that same riot, or any crisis for that matter, you'd immediately look to Clint for guidance and protection. It's the same for dogs. If something happens to cause fear or uncertainty, and the dog does not have what he perceives as a strong leader, he is more likely to try to take the situation into his own paws.

Unfortunately, whether through books, the media, well-intentioned friends, or ill-informed trainers, many owners have gotten the idea that leadership can be achieved by physically dominating a dog. If you've ever had the opportunity to observe a pack of wolves, you might have noticed that the "alpha"—the leader—does not bully the other wolves or force them onto their backs. The latter technique was used many years ago by some trainers and has resurfaced as of late, but it does not convey the message some think it does. The "alpha roll," as it is commonly called, was based on a wolf study in which scientists believed that a wolf would roll another wolf on his back to dominate him. It was later discovered that this information was incorrect—but somehow that part didn't make it to the general public. If a wolf rolls another onto his back, he probably means to kill that wolf. When you see one wolf on his back with another standing over him, in most cases, the subordinate placed *himself* in that position. So if your clients are using the alpha roll, take a moment to explain why the technique is not appropriate or scientifically valid, and that dogs most certainly do not mistake people for other dogs, regardless of how a hand is curled or what body language or vocalizations are being used!

> True leaders do not need to prove a thing; it's the middle-ranking pack members who are always squabbling for status.

Leadership is established through a combination of controlling valued resources, asking a dog to earn them (what many trainers refer to as a "Nothing in Life is Free" program), and acting in a way that exudes authority and confidence. Let's imagine our friend Clint Eastwood walking a fear-reactive dog down the street. No doubt he would calmly and quietly let the dog know the expected course of action, and maneuver him past any potential hazards safely. Through practice, the dog would eventually no longer have the need to react toward other dogs. You might not want to tell your owners that they should strive for Clint-inspired mannerisms— we can't have an army of Dirty Harry housewives marching their dogs down the block!—but they should be coached to strive for that calm, self-assured quality.

You may be wondering what exactly an owner should expect a reactive dog to do instead in a situation that would normally provoke an aggressive display. Although the answer will differ depending on the specific situation, there are certain skills that will come in handy across the board. We'll take a look at those next.

1 Hart. B.L., and Eckstein, R.A., 1997. The role of gonadal hormones in the occurrence of objectionable behaviors in dogs and cats. *Applied Animal Behaviour Science* 52; 331-344

2 O'Farrell, V.O. and Peachey, E., 1990. Behavioural effects of ovariohysterectomy on bitches. *J. Small Anim. Pract.* 31: 595-598

16

Skills to Teach

With complicated or severe aggression cases, it is sometimes necessary to spend the entire initial session gathering detailed information. But in most cases, once you have taken a thorough history, presented a summary of the dog's issues and how you will address them, and established that the client is willing and able to carry out the proposed behavior modification plan, the next step will be to discuss techniques and teach skills.

The following is an overview of some techniques and skills that are commonly used in treating various types of aggression. Of course, your choice of which ones to use will depend on the individual situation.

Classical Conditioning

Walter is a year-and-a-half-old Scottish terrier who lunges wildly at other dogs on walks—and not in a friendly, I-can't-wait-to-meet-you way. If Walter so much as spies another dog at a distance, he gets so worked up that his owner Molly has a hard time holding him back, never mind getting his attention. When that happens Molly could shout, "Free sirloin for life!" and Walter wouldn't respond. While that might frustrate Molly, the truth is, in his highly aroused state, Walter is *unable* to respond. His system is flooded with adrenalin and other stress hormones, and he is literally not capable of mentally processing his owner's requests.

Rather than setting Walter up for failure by expecting him to perform a skill when he is so aroused, you might recommend that Molly begin by using classical conditioning. In this case, you would pair something Walter likes—food—with the presence of other dogs. Naturally, you would start at a distance that does not trigger a reaction, and gradually work in closer proximity to other dogs.

When using treats for classical conditioning, the owner should begin calmly but rapidly feeding tidbits, one after another, at the moment the trigger appears. The treating may be accompanied by chatting in a happy tone of voice if desired. At the moment the trigger disappears, so do the happy talk and treats. (If Walter were more toy-motivated than food-motivated, a toy could be substituted for food by allowing Walter to tug at it or hold it in his mouth briefly while the trigger was present.) This pairing technique sounds simple and straightforward, but very few lay people get the timing right at first.

Have your clients practice classical conditioning exercises indoors first, away from the presence of the trigger. For example, ask the owner to stand with the dog on leash, treats at the ready. Position yourself so you can appear and disappear around a corner. Instruct the owner to start chatting and giving treats when you appear, and to stop immediately the moment you disappear. Because the owner may be nervous, and probably has not practiced this technique before, her timing may be a bit off at first. That's okay; it will improve over time.

Classical conditioning simply creates an association between two things. In this case, the dog already has a negative association with one of the items—other dogs—so technically, you are using *counterconditioning* to change the dog's emotional reaction to the trigger. You are *conditioning* a reaction that is *counter* to, or incompatible with, the established one. Think of counterconditoning as a subset of classical conditioning.

In our indoor practice scenario the owner was stationary, which made mastering the timing of treat presentation easier. In other words, just like the dogs you train, you have set your client up to succeed by breaking the task down into small steps. You could make it even easier at first if necessary by not having the dog on leash (as long as the dog is not human-aggressive).

Once your client's timing is precise, remain indoors but role-play what will happen once you venture outdoors. Tell the client that when you appear from around the corner this time, you will start walking toward her. Her job will be to walk toward and then pass you with her dog on leash while remaining relaxed, treating and chatting happily as soon as the dog sees you, stopping the treats and chatting once you have passed each other.

Although it might seem silly to act out a scene in someone's living room, practicing in a safe environment first, where there is no danger of an actual encounter, is invaluable. It helps the person to get comfortable with the exercise without the added stress of the presence of the trigger. It builds muscle memory on the part of the owner, and gives the dog practice at paying attention to her.

Another technique that can be extremely useful when working with a dog-aggressive dog, assuming he has a strong bond with the owner, is abandonment. In this scenario, the owner seemingly disappears when the dog reacts to another dog. (The exercise is done in a safe manner using long lines, leashes, and careful planning.) The dog is rewarded for walking non-reactively past another dog, and punished (by loss of the owner's presence) for reacting. The dog soon learns to pass other dogs calmly. (To learn more about this method, see *Resources* for Trish King's "Abandonment Training" DVD.)

Operant Conditioning and Obedience Skills

In cases where a dog is already able to focus on his owner in the presence of the trigger (which may be possible immediately, or only after a time of working with classical conditioning, depending on the severity of the problem), very often you will use operant conditioning. That simply means that the dog is actually expected to *do* something when the trigger appears in order to earn the reward. In other words, you are helping your client to teach her dog a substitute behavior for lunging, barking, or whatever other undesirable behavior is being displayed. You will find that the following skills make for extremely useful substitute behaviors in many situations.

Attention

A dog's ability to pay attention—to make eye contact with his owner when his name is called—is crucial in many types of aggression cases. Staring at another dog is often one of the first links in the chain of behaviors that leads to biting. If that link is removed, the escalation of arousal can be interrupted and the situation defused. Remember, few dogs bite without warning, although it might appear that way to the untrained eye. Perhaps a dog's reaction toward other dogs normally starts with a stiffening of the body, lowered head, and hard stare. If the dog's owner can be taught to notice those signals and get the dog to focus on her instead, she will then be able to remove him from the situation calmly, or refocus him on another activity.

Touch

Touch, also called targeting, is a skill that can effectively maintain focus and keep a dog in cognitive mode rather than allowing arousal levels to spiral out of control. For our purposes, targeting means that upon hearing the verbal cue, "Touch!" the dog will touch his nose to the back of the owner's hand. Going back to Walter, let's say Molly has worked with him to the point where he can now pass other dogs without lunging at them; in fact, when he sees another dog, he now looks to Molly for a treat instead. This is an improvement, but giving Walter something more physically active to do will channel all that arousal into an acceptable action, which will be easier for him than simply remaining focused on his owner.

Molly can now call Walter's name to get his attention, and then ask him to perform touches as they pass the other dog. Touch can also be useful for dogs who become nervous (and therefore potentially dangerous) at the vet's office. Your clients can have their dogs do touches in the waiting room and, if the vet allows, even during the examination. Touch is one of my favorite skills, as it is fast and easy to teach both dogs and people, and is useful in a variety of situations.

Walk-Aways

In some scenarios, especially those in which a trigger appears unexpectedly, removing the dog from the environment is often the best course of action. For example, you are working with a program of desensitization where a dog is learning to gradually tolerate the presence of other dogs at progressively nearer distances. Suddenly, a dog appears from around a corner; it surprises both you and your client's dog. If you weren't prepared for such a situation it could turn into a confrontation or, at the least, set your progress back. The walk-away is the perfect solution for just such a circumstance. It's simple: all the dog is required to do is to follow the owner in another direction, away from the trigger. The verbal cue should be sharp and repetitive; for example, "Hey, hey, hey!" followed by calmly walking the dog away from the trigger. The walk-away prevents the owner from having to drag the dog, which would only engage the dog's oppositional reflex, making him want to pull even harder. The walk-away should be practiced in all directions, eventually including a complete about-turn. Have your client practice first in the home with no distractions, then outdoors with as few distractions as possible, so she will be prepared to get her dog safely and calmly out of the area should an unexpected situation arise.

An important ingredient for the success of any behavior modification program involving reactivity in public places is for the owner to become aware of the environment. Teach your clients to get in the habit of diligently scanning the streets for other dogs or people (depending on what triggers the dog's reactivity). This vigilance should not be a nervous, furtive glancing around, but a calm, confident awareness. This will allow the owner to get the dog's attention and then do a walk-away or whatever else is necessary while the window of opportunity is still open, before the dog becomes so highly aroused that he cannot respond.

Settle

Settle is more a state of mind than a specific position. When a dog is settled he feels calm, whether he happens to be lying on his side or in a relaxed down with his weight over on one hip. The goal of "settle" is simply that, on your cue, the dog assumes a position that is accompanied by a feeling of relaxation.

There are several good reasons to teach dogs with aggression issues how to settle. First, feeling relaxed is at odds with feeling aggressive; just try to experience both at once! Just as with people, the more relaxed a dog is in everyday life, the less likely aggression is to be an issue. It's a sad fact that, like some people, some dogs really do not know *how* to relax. Those are the dogs whose energy levels, on a scale of one to ten, always seem to be at eleven. For dogs who are often stressed, reactive, or just "tightly wound" in general, teaching them to relax is a kindness.

Once a dog understands the "settle" cue, it can be used in certain situations where mild aggression is an issue. For example, a dog who is nervous around visitors and may snap defensively can be taught to settle in a safe place away from foot traffic, such as a dog bed on the far side of the room. This approach not only keeps everyone safe, but also helps the dog to associate the presence of strangers with feelings of relaxation.

Instructions for teaching attention, touch, walk-aways, and settle can be found in my book *Help for Your Fearful Dog*, as well as a variety of obedience training books and DVDs.

Other Skills

Regardless of the type of aggression, basic obedience skills should be rock-solid. A dog who chases and bites children who are running and playing in the back yard can't be chasing them and doing a down-stay at the same time. A dog who nips at visitors at the front door can't be lunging at them and going to his bed at the far end of the room at the same time. In short, the more control the owner has over the dog's behavior via learned skills, the better the chances that the dog can be instructed to perform, or even offer, a behavior that is incompatible with aggression.

In addition to the aforementioned skills, as well as basic obedience behaviors such as sit, down, stay, come, and walk nicely on leash, you may choose to teach others, depending on the situation. For example, if the issue involves a dog snapping at his owners whenever they try to remove him from the couch, teaching "off" would be useful (along with the dog dragging a long line indoors so no one has to grab his collar). If a dog tends to guard access to locations from a canine housemate by lying across doorways, instilling a strong recall so the owner can call him away from the area would be useful. With a dog who resource guards, "leave it" (meaning "Don't even think about putting your mouth on that thing") and "drop it" (in other words, "Kindly spit that thing out so I don't have to chase you around the house like a lunatic to get it back") are helpful skills that can assist clients in preventing conflicts.

Spatially-oriented cues are helpful as well. "Back up" is a useful conflict-avoidance behavior, as a dog walking backward on a verbal cue effectively removes him from the person's space without their having to make physical contact. Another helpful skill to teach is "away," meaning the dog should leave the area.

At the first session with a new client, because of the time-consuming aspect of taking a history and reviewing management and other vital topics, you may end up only teaching one or two skills. Regardless of which ones you introduce, always do the following:

1. Explain each exercise and how it will be used to solve the problematic behavior.

2. As you teach the skill to the dog, explain to the owner step by step what you are doing.

3. Once the dog has the idea, let the client practice as you repeat the instructions.

This three-step process is critical. By the end of the session, the client should understand the exercise and get the dog to perform it successfully. Emphasize the importance of working with the dog a few times daily for short periods so the skills can be put to use at the next session.

Ending the Session

Always end the session by asking whether there are any questions about the material that was covered, the skills that were taught, or how to practice between lessons. Then schedule a follow-up appointment. If the initial session was spent taking an in-depth history and no skills were taught, set the follow-up date as soon as you'd like, since no practice time is needed. In cases where you have taught a skill or two, a week to two weeks later is fine. If you have recommended major lifestyle changes and a comprehensive behavior modification program that includes classical or operant conditioning exercises, schedule the next lesson three weeks ahead to leave enough time to gauge changes in the dog's behavior.

Remind your clients to call if there are any questions between sessions. It is important that they feel comfortable doing so, as one quick piece of advice from you can help ensure that everything is going according to plan, thereby smoothing the way for further progress. Consider creating a tickle file (or setting up prompts on your computer) to remind yourself to call the client midway before the next session to check in.

Written Assessment and Follow-Up Letter

Written Assessment

After you have completed the initial session, write up an assessment. Try to do this as soon as possible after the session so the information will be fresh in your mind. You could sit in your vehicle afterwards and scribble notes, type them into a laptop computer, or speak them into a mini-recorder for later transcription. This summary need not adhere to any particular format, but should contain basic information about the dog and the household (for example, whether the environment was particularly chaotic, not, "That shag carpet was *so* seventies!"), a summary of the dog's major and secondary issues, what was covered at the session, the proposed behavior modification plan, your prognosis, and any other information you feel is important. Jot down brief notes after each subsequent session as well. These summaries should be kept in your files for future reference.

Follow-Up Letter for Clients

In addition to the written assessment you create for your own records, send a version of it as a follow-up letter to your client. I say a "version" of it because if you have a note to yourself about, say, how one family member seems to have a Neanderthal mentality about how the dog should be trained, that's not exactly the type of professional opinion your clients need to see. Something more along the lines of "modern approaches to training were discussed" would be more appropriate.

Sending a follow-up letter demonstrates that you are organized and efficient, and lets your clients know that their dog's welfare is on your mind even after the session has ended. Because it offers a summary of the issues and lays out a treatment plan, the letter can help an owner to grasp the full picture more easily. Being able to actually hold the plan in their hands helps owners to feel that the problem is workable. Another advantage is that if any family members were absent during the session, they can read your recommendations rather than hearing the information secondhand.

In cases where you feel that a client does not truly understand the severity of the problem or what it will take to address it, send an extra copy of the follow-up letter to be signed and returned. The signature indicates that the person has read the letter, understands the information, and agrees to participate as instructed in the proposed behavior modification plan. This letter should have specific requirements such as "Shasta will be walked twice daily, 20-30 minutes per walk," and "Meals will be changed from free-feeding to two meals per day, with the dish picked up after fifteen minutes if the food has not been eaten." The very act of signing and returning the letter may engender more compliance. The letter also gives you something to refer back to should there be any future confusion regarding the severity of the dog's issues, the effort required on the part of the owner, or what was discussed.

Veterinary Letter

You might also want to send a post-session letter to the client's veterinarian. If the vet referred the client to you, sending a well-constructed assessment shows your professionalism, and keeps the vet abreast of the dog's behavioral prognosis and progress. If the client's vet was not the original referral source, there is no need to send the letter unless you are recommending that medication be discussed, or if the behavior might affect the veterinary staff, such as the dog having handling issues that require muzzling to prevent bites. Regardless of whether the vet was the referring party, do not send this letter without your client's permission! The vast majority of clients I have dealt with have not objected, and most appreciated that professionals were working as a team to help their dog.

Sample Assessment for Your Records

On the following pages is a sample assessment written after the first session with a new client whose dogs were fighting in the home, as well as a follow-up assessment written after a subsequent session. These are the type of informal summaries you would keep for your own records.

Session Date: 5/15
Clients: Bill and Stacey Warner (no kids)

Dogs:

"Mimi"   F 2 yrs. black Lab, intact (breeder for Guide Dogs)
"Coco"   F 6 yrs. choc. Lab, spayed
"Rosie"   F 4 yr. black Lab, spayed
"Riley"   M 7.5 yr. yellow Lab, neutered

Reason for Consultation: Fighting between Mimi and Coco

Health/Nutrition/Exercise: No health issues. All dogs are fed Wellness dry food and walked one to two times daily, together. Average 30-45 minutes per walk. Dogs all sleep in living room, no crates, and are kept in the yard when no one is home.

History: Mimi was obtained at the age of seven months. Another owner was raising her for Guide Dogs, but decided she would be a breeder instead. Coco and the other two dogs were already in the home (had been from young pups). All three original dogs get along well. Per Stacey, whenever a new dog is adopted, Coco "growls and puts them in their place."

There has been friction between Coco and Mimi from the beginning. Fights began after Mimi was in the home for a month. Although skirmishes and low-level fights happen once every few days, only two fights have resulted in injuries requiring vet visits, both to treat Coco. The usual pattern is Coco taking exception to something Mimi does, whether coming close when Coco has a toy, or even when she has nothing and is just lying there (advised to look for subtle signals, e.g., hard eye). Two fights have been near doorways or when going through them (controlling access to location). Coco growls, Mimi then jumps on Coco's back and won't let go. Coco is always the injured party. Damage included a torn ear, and on a separate vet visit, injury to her side (five stitches required).

Mimi was sent to Guide Dogs for breeding in early May – home 5/20. Advised to keep her separated from Coco until our visit a few days later.

Mimi goes to work with Stacey most days. No problems upon Mimi's return. But some problems after extended absences, e.g., when Mimi is sent off for breeding.
- Mimi and Coco will play together, rest together, etc. Fights *only* break out in owners' presence. Dogs are left alone together when owners gone.

- All dogs are walked together. Coco is reactive with unfamiliar dogs on walks. She is being walked on a choke chain. When she reacts, Bill says, "Don't worry" but then corrects her with choke chain. This stress carries over to home life with dogs she *can* take it out on.

Recommendations:

1. Reduce Coco's stress levels on walks. We fitted her for a Gentle Leader. I showed them how to use it. Owners already know how to teach targeting nose to back of hand (they do clicker training in agility class with Rosie). They will teach Coco this skill so we can use it when she encounters other dogs on walks. They will brush up on her attention skills. Advised to walk Coco separately for now. Do longer walks if possible for all dogs.

2. Food and chew bones are major triggers. Dogs are currently all fed in the yard at a distance from each other. Recommended instead to separate Coco and Mimi at feeding time (one indoors, one out). Separate for bones as well. If all dogs need to be indoors, can tether Coco and Mimi at a distance from each other with bones, preferably out of each other's sight.

3. As doorways are trigger points, more order is needed when going in and out. Owners should practice having dogs sit first, then call each one through. (All dogs already have an excellent level of obedience training.) Owners have two separate doors going in and out of yard to use if necessary.

4. After a long absence when Mimi comes home—especially since she smells different due to breeding, etc.—spray all dogs with lavender, etc. so they all smell alike (lavender also calming), be extra vigilant.

5. Identified Coco's escalation signals. Hard eye, stiffening body are first signs. Progresses to agonistic pucker, then growl. At first signs, Stacey and Bill should both stand up, lightly say, "Too bad!" and leave the room. As dogs only fight/posture in owners' presence, status by association (or guarding valued resource—owner) is removed. Coco should learn that every time she starts, she loses her backup (or valued resource). Owners feel they can do this safely and the situation would not escalate once they have left the room. Also discussed the possibility of keeping house lines on the dogs if necessary as a safety measure so they could easily be separated in the event of a fight.

6. Recommended that sometimes, instead of abandonment, they use a calm, pleasant tone of voice to ask both dogs to go to their beds to lie down. Also advised Bill to stop using the phrase "Don't worry" in conjunction with corrections on walks.

7. Notice Mimi's body language too, look for stress signals or less obvious threats toward Coco. Recommended books/DVDs to learn more about subtle stress signals and body language.

8. Leadership program and continued practice of obedience skills for all dogs.

Prognosis is good for both dogs to stay in the home, so long as owners follow the program. Bill and Stacey now understand that although they thought Mimi was the problem since she was inflicting the damage, Coco is actually the one starting the fights. Although female-female aggression can be extremely challenging, Coco gives obvious signals with progressive escalation, and fights only occur in the owners' presence. Owners are intelligent and committed and likely to follow through. Will follow up in one week, work on Coco's issues toward other dogs on walks (using Gentle Leader and touch command, or possibly abandonment), and adjust plan as necessary.

Follow-Up Session: 5/23

One day last week, Stacey brought Coco to her parents' house. Her parents have two dogs, a female Lab mix and a male spaniel mix. No fights to date, although there was some posturing and air snapping when Coco positioned near Stacey and the Lab mix approached. This time, Stacey paid careful attention to Coco's precursors to aggression. Family was in the living room with the dogs, Stacey on couch, Coco lying at Stacey's feet. At Coco's first signal—growl—Stacey stood up and lightly said, "Oops, gotta go!" and walked out of the room. Coco immediately stopped growling and followed her. When they returned two minutes later, no further tension.

Stacey and Bill have been careful about doorways and letting the dogs in and out separately. Will be hypervigilant, as Mimi may be pregnant. Abandonment technique worked during the week at their home, and "jolly routine" and go to bed did too. Much less tension at home. Walk times have increased.

We took Coco for a walk—doing well on Gentle Leader. Practiced having her target Stacey's hand on trails where neighborhood dogs are walked. I walked Coco at the start of the session, and we saw another dog. Did touches about 10 feet from the other dog as it passed. Coco acted like she barely noticed that the other dog was there, though she had definitely seen it. Stacey and Bill each took turns practicing, both did well. They have good instincts. Both are very pleased with the Gentle Leader (we also fit one on Rosie to control pulling on their separate walks) and will continue to use it, along with the targeting hand technique.

They will practice for the next few weeks and let me know how things are going.

Sample Veterinary Letter and Assessment

You can see how the preceding letter could be adapted for clients by leaving out the notes to yourself and comments about the clients, and focusing strictly on what was done and what needs to be changed or addressed. On the following pages is an example of a more formal type of report (from a different case) that might be sent to a referring veterinarian, along with a sample cover letter:

Dear Dr. Polk,

I recently visited Ellen and Rodney Tamaka's home to do a behavior modification session with Yoshi, their fifteen-month-old Shiba Inu. I thought you might like to see the notes from our session, along with my recommendations to the family.

Thank you for entrusting your clients to our care; your confidence in us is much appreciated. Please let me know if you have any questions about Yoshi's case. You can reach me at 661-555-2225 or via email at dogtrainer@provider.com.

Sincerely,
Nicole Wilde
Gentle Guidance Dog Training

CLIENT

Name: **Ellen and Rodney Tamaka**
Address: **313 Wayside Lane, Palmdale, CA 91399**
Phone: **661-555-1177**
Family: **Son Donny 13 yrs., daughter Linda 11 yrs.**

DOG

Name: **Yoshi**
Breed: **Shiba Inu**
Age: **15 months**
Sex: **Male**
Neut: **Yes**

PRESENTING ISSUE: Aggression toward family members.

- Yoshi will bite if his paws are touched.
- Problem with Linda putting a body harness on Yoshi for daily walks because she must lift his paws through the nylon loops.
- Yoshi will bite if he does not want to be moved or handled, such as on the couch.
- Yoshi will bite anyone if approached when he is under the kitchen table.
- Owners have tried on numerous occasions, on the advice of the breeder, to use force to subdue Yoshi and "show him who's boss." This always resulted in escalated arousal and an aggressive display.
- Yoshi gives warning before biting: lip curl, may snarl, air snap.
- Yoshi gets "puppy zoomies" nightly, races around the house.
- Must be muzzled for veterinary exams. It has become increasingly difficult for Ellen or Rodney to place a muzzle on him.

BACKGROUND:

Origin: Yoshi was obtained as a pup from a breeder (Karen Kasalian, Stormsong Shibas) at the age of eight weeks.

Medical: No known medical problems or food allergies. Not currently on any medication. Last veterinary exam was nine months ago. Yoshi was neutered at six months of age.

Nutrition: Yoshi is fed twice daily, low-quality supermarket brand dry food. Ellen adds scrambled eggs, cheese and other goodies whenever Yoshi does not eat. If Rodney is home with Yoshi, he feeds dry food alone and Yoshi eats it.

Exercise: Yoshi is taken for walks at least four times weekly, primarily by Ellen, using a standard type of body harness and a 4-ft. leash. Walks last twenty minutes average and do not tire Yoshi.

Training: Yoshi knows "sit," and Linda has taught him some tricks. They attended a chain store training class when Yoshi was a pup. He does not have a solid recall, no "down," and "stay" is so-so. Response to request for attention is poor.

Logistics: Yoshi sleeps in bed with Ellen and Rodney. When they are away from home, he is kept in the yard.

INCIDENTS:

1. Yoshi bit Ellen two months ago when she was sitting in the family room on the floor brushing him. She had been brushing for approximately ten minutes with no reaction. Ellen said she might have brushed too close to his rear, where he is sensitive. Yoshi bit Ellen on the hand and broke the skin. Slight tear due to Ellen pulling away; no puncture.

2. Approximately a month ago, Yoshi bit Ellen on the hand when she tried to move him from where he was sitting on the couch. (Yoshi likes to sit on top of the couch and look out the front window, and has always been allowed to do so.) The bite broke the skin. One tear resulted from Ellen pulling away; no puncture.

3.   Yoshi Bit Rodney in bed approximately one month ago; he has done so numerous times—five or six by Rodney's estimate. He will bite Rodney if he tries to move Yoshi in bed or if the blanket is moved around him. Bites are firm enough to cause bruising; no tears.

4.   Two weeks ago, Yoshi bit Donny on the hand when Donny tried to pick up a piece of bread from the floor that Yoshi (unbeknownst to Donny) was guarding. No broken skin, no bruising.

5.   Last week, Yoshi bit Donny when Donny was sitting on the floor under the kitchen table and got too close to Yoshi. Exact circumstances are unknown; no one observed the bite. Bite was to Donny's forearm; there was a slight tear as he pulled away.

6.   Yoshi has also bitten Linda in similar circumstances to #4; no tear or puncture.

The family has been living with Yoshi's behavior since the age of approximately seven months. They have learned to avoid some of the things Yoshi does not like, but have become accustomed to being snarled and snapped at on a daily basis. We discussed that this is not normal behavior and that they do not realize how much they have come to accept the aberrant behavior.

RECOMMENDATIONS:

1.   Rule out medical causes of aggression – get full blood panel and full thyroid panel in addition to thorough physical exam and whatever else their veterinarian recommends.

2.   Immediate management is key. Therefore, Yoshi is no longer allowed to sleep in bed with Ellen and Rodney. Since he has a crate he will go into easily, he will sleep crated. If getting him into the crate becomes an issue (because of Yoshi's handling issues), he can sleep in the gated laundry room or a similar area. At home, Yoshi will wear a "house line" (a 4-foot leash with the loop cut off), so that if he must be moved, it can be done without confrontation. (Showed them proper human body

language and attitude when using a house line.) For now, they will avoid handling Yoshi's paws or rear.

3. Yoshi will be walked using the Easy Walk body harness, which Ellen can place on him and remove easily without having to handle his paws. She will aim for daily walks, gradually increasing the duration to at least 30-45 minutes, and will try to fit in a second walk after work.

4. Implement leadership program as described on handout (e.g., must sit to earn food, walks, etc.).

5. Children are not allowed to take Yoshi for walks without a parent present. They have been advised to stay away from underneath table, and if Yoshi is showing any threatening behavior, to call a parent.

6. Ellen and Rodney will begin to desensitize Yoshi to wearing a muzzle per my instructions. This will make veterinary exams, as well as visits to the groomer, safer. We will also use the muzzle to begin exercises to desensitize Yoshi to being handled.

7. Change food to California Natural (better ingredients, low protein). Ellen is not to add food once kibble is offered. If she wants to give eggs, etc., will present with food, not after kibble is refused. Will give Yoshi 15 minutes to eat, then remove food. (Use safe handling techniques as discussed.)

8. Ellen will approach Yoshi while he is eating kibble (moving gradually closer over time), to toss bits of cheese or other better-than-kibble treats. Ellen practiced this at our session and Yoshi did well. Also showed the couple another technique to begin to work on resource guarding. (Parents only to do these exercises, then once progress is made, children to do exercises safely and supervised.)

FURTHER RECOMMENDATIONS:

Desensitization/counterconditioning protocols to address handling issues (rear and paws, and being moved). A protocol will also be implemented to address the resource guarding behavior. Attempt to lower stress levels through more exercise and improved diet. Leadership program. Yoshi's current low triggering threshold and general stress level indicate that if no progress is made within a reasonable time frame, the assistance of medication could be advised in conjunction with behavior modification protocols.

PROGNOSIS:

Positive: Ellen and Rodney realize the gravity of the situation and that rehoming is not an option. They are aware that the alternative to behavior modification at this point is euthanasia. They manage the situation when their children's friends come to visit by putting Yoshi in an inaccessible area. The family can avoid being bitten most of the time since they know the triggers so well. Yoshi has never attempted to bite anyone outside of the family, although this is probably because those people did not do any of the things that trigger the aggression. A major plus is that although Yoshi has bitten, he does show bite inhibition, as demonstrated by bruising and tears as opposed to puncture wounds.

Negative: There have been many incidents and a certain level of denial by the family as to the severity of the situation. Cooperation is not one hundred percent from all family members at all times on rules such as leaving Yoshi alone in certain situations (e.g., when he has something in his possession). This is especially of concern because of the children.

Ellen and Rodney will make a veterinary appointment within the week.

~ * ~ * ~ * ~ * ~ * ~ * ~ *

In addition to sending a follow-up letter to the client, and an assessment to the vet if warranted, call the client midway before your next appointment to check on progress and find out whether there are any questions. Clients are often hesitant to call for fear of being a bother, but these issues are too important to let questions go unanswered. As previously mentioned, checking in allows you to answer queries and to ensure that the protocols you laid out are being followed. It also affords the opportunity to tweak a protocol if necessary. In the case of a serious aggression issue, you might give a follow-up call between each session, especially if those sessions are separated by more than a week's time.

18

Follow-Up Sessions

Before we discuss how to structure follow-up sessions, a caution: If you did not feel it was safe to have the dog in the room during the initial session, remind your client to have him contained before your arrival this time as well. Hopefully you will be able to work directly with the dog at this session, but take your time, and always take measures to ensure your safety.

Review

Begin each follow-up session by having a brief chat to gauge progress, make adjustments to the program as needed, and clarify any confusion. First, ask whether the client has any questions and, if so, take a few moments to address each one. Then ask whether there have been any incidents involving aggression or reactivity since the previous session. If there were incidents, get as many details as possible. Discuss what happened, how it was handled, and what might be done to prevent it from happening again. Adjust your behavior modification program if necessary based on the information you obtain.

For each topic or behavior you taught at the preceding session, ask for a brief progress report. You need to know what's working and what's not, and if you don't ask point by point, the client might not offer all the pertinent information. There's no need to make it sound like an interrogation, but your questions should be specific. For example, imagine that you are working with a client whose dog is reactive to other dogs in public. You previously offered suggestions for making daily walks a calmer event, which included using a head halter, and doing walk-aways if necessary. If you phrase the question, "How have the walks been going?" the client, perhaps feeling that the dog is less reactive than before, might simply answer, "Better." On the other hand, asking how the dog reacts when seeing other dogs now that he's wearing the head halter might yield the response, "Actually, whenever he sees another dog, he starts trying to paw it off. What should I do about that?" By asking specifically whether any walk-aways were necessary, you might get the answer, "Yes, actually, a dog surprised us and I was able to get Sierra to follow me with no problem. It was great!" Or, "Well, I tried it but Sierra was already lunging at the other dog. I just wasn't watching and didn't see it coming, so I wasn't sure what to do." The latter answer offers an opportunity to review your previous instructions about remaining alert on walks.

If you gave management instructions at the first session, follow up on those as well. For example, if you had instructed the client that for the time being, the dog should be contained in another room whenever visitors are present, check whether the client had any visitors and whether the dog was contained. Whether discussing management or behavior, be sure to praise your clients for compliance and a job well done. Offering positive reinforcement to your human students is just as important as giving it to your canine pupils, not only to let them know that they are doing a good job, but to keep them motivated.

The verbal review should take only five to ten minutes. To wrap up, ask whether there is anything else you need to know. Although there might not have been any incidents since the last session, that last question could bring up anything from the dog having growled at someone (and the client didn't consider that an "incident") to questions about a new issue that was not covered during the first session.

Assess Skills and Progress

If you have taught specific skills, ask the client to demonstrate them with the dog. Asking whether the skills have been practiced is not enough; you need to see that the dog and owner can reliably accomplish them together. If the skills are not being performed at the level they need to be in order to move forward, make adjustments as necessary.

If the client has not practiced the skills or implemented your suggestions, find out why. Life happens, and it is possible that there was a sick child at home that week who needed the owner's full attention; or that things were extremely busy at the person's job. In those cases, a lack of progress is unfortunate, but understandable.

If you arrive session after session to find that the person has not practiced, see if you can get to the root of the problem. *Ask* what the problem is, and help to find creative solutions. If the person continually gets too overwhelmed with everyday life to find time to practice, see if you can come up with a way to fit the training into their daily routine, or break it down into smaller, more manageable pieces. Alternately, if you also offer training where you come to the home a few times a week to work with the dog without the owner present, or offer board-and-train, discuss those possibilities as ways to jump-start the process.

If the person is just not motivated, find out why. Perhaps another family member is the one who wanted the training, but can't be present at sessions, leaving the person doing the sessions feeling resentful. Or maybe the person doesn't realize the severity of the problem, in which case a frank discussion is in order. Whatever the reason, be direct but compassionate, and help find a solution. You *must* have compliance in order to make progress.

Put Skills into Practice

If the client/dog team is performing well together, this is the time to put the skills that have been taught into practice. For example, the client and her dog-aggressive dog have mastered the assigned skills of "attention" and "touch." You can now work with the dog outdoors. The goal will be for the dog to pay attention to his owner when asked, as well as to touch a hand when cued. This will be done first in a low-traffic area with no distractions, then with other dogs at a distance. Over the course of subsequent sessions, you will gradually work closer to other dogs.

Of course, your progress will be dictated by the dog's behavior. With some dogs, one or two sessions will yield vast improvements; with others, it may take weeks or possibly even months, depending on the severity of the behavior and how long the dog has had the issue. Always keep your clients focused on the overall behavioral goal. Pointing out incremental successes along the way can help keep them motivated.

For dogs who are highly aggressive toward strangers or other dogs in public, use a basket muzzle. If the client has not acclimated the dog to the muzzle as instructed, you will have to decide whether to put off working around the dog's trigger until the next session, to put the muzzle on the dog anyway, or to work without one. This decision should be based on the dog's temperament and the particular situation. If you are using a head halter as well as a basket muzzle, the halter should be placed on the dog first, with the muzzle over it. *Always check the equipment on the client's dog, even if it is a simple buckle collar.* Be sure everything is fitted correctly and nothing is frayed, chewed, or showing signs of potential breakage.

Employing Your Own Dog

If a dog is aggressive toward other dogs, it is handy to have a dog of your own to bring along to the session. That way you can work the client's dog around another dog without having to rely on dogs you encounter on the street or in the park whose temperaments are unknown to you. There is no point in working a dog-reactive dog around a dog who may respond to his presence by lunging and growling at him, thereby arousing him even further.

For your dog to be a good candidate for this type of work, he must be "bombproof." In other words, he will not react, no matter how reactive another dog becomes. Of course, you will keep your dog absolutely safe not only by checking the equipment on the client's dog for fit and security, but by keeping your own dog stationary (tied to a tree or fence, for example) while *you* work the client's dog.

I would never trust my own dog's safety to the handling skills of an average pet owner, and neither should you. Eventually the client will need to work her dog herself, but by the time you allow this you will have gotten the dog far enough along that it will be safe. A good practice to implement when the client is working her dog is to attach a second leash to the collar or harness that *you* will hold, just in case.

When using your own dog, take care to make the event a pleasant experience. I used to play fetch with Soko, my ball-obsessed German shepherd, after each session so she would associate the sessions with something she loved. Use whatever your dog enjoys after each session, and always monitor stress signals. If your dog starts to become stressed or reactive, rethink the arrangement. The day Soko—ten years old and starting to feel her arthritis—reacted to another dog was the day she retired.

So what can you do if you are working with a dog who has dog-aggression issues, but you don't have your own dog to bring along? I'm currently in that position. Soko was my bombproof dog. Dogs could bark, lunge, and sing the Star-Spangled Banner for all she cared—she never reacted. Unfortunately, Soko passed away last year, and although my other dog Mojo is still with us, he is over fourteen years old and in no condition to work.

If you do not have a workable dog, get creative. Very often in a typical suburban neighborhood, there will be plenty of dogs behind fences— and believe me, your clients will know exactly where each one lives. You can work the dog while passing these homes at a distance, then eventually closer. Any area with enough space where you know other people walk their dogs is a good choice. Ensure everyone's safety by working at a distance that the dog can handle, then gradually move closer as the dog's responses improve. You can even stand in the parking lot of a pet supply store or doggy daycare and work at a distance as people get in and out of cars, and disappear and reappear from stores.

Indoor Practice

Depending on the type of aggression, you might not work outdoors at all. If the dog is fine with people on the street but aggressive toward visitors, working outdoors isn't going to help. Instead, engage the skills that were taught at the first session. Perhaps you had taught "Go to your place." The goal is that whenever a visitor enters the home, the dog will go to his bed, lie down, and stay. Once the dog has mastered going to his place on cue, it's time to practice in a real-life situation. Refrain from using neighbors and friends as bait! Instead, *you* play the part of the stranger. Sure, the dog has already met you, but that's not important. What *is* important is that the dog gets accustomed to the pattern of the doorbell ringing, hearing the owner give the cue, and then going to bed, lying down, and staying. You will gradually progress to familiar visitors, and eventually to people who are unfamiliar to the dog. Always stress the incremental aspect of building on small successes and not rushing the process.

Whatever type of work you do at follow-up sessions, always take a few minutes at the end to sit down and chat with the client. Summarize what was covered at the lesson, reiterate the most important points, and allow the client to make notes. Ask whether there are any questions, then review what should be practiced before the next lesson, including exactly how and how often to practice. Remind your clients that, as always, they should contact you if an incident occurs or if questions arise between then and the next scheduled session. (By this time you might be envisioning receiving pestering phone calls night and day if you keep extending this offer, but in my experience, it just doesn't happen.)

When to Terminate Training

The most common reason to terminate training is because the dog's issues have been resolved. If you have sold a package of sessions, assuming the problem has been addressed, when to terminate training will be obvious. If you are seeing clients on a per-session basis, it's not as straightforward. Your decision should be based on two things: how the dog is performing, and how the client feels about the dog's behavior. Obviously, if the dog is still reactive with other dogs or people, more work is needed. But in some cases, although the dog has made major progress, the client will still need a bit of hand-holding in order to feel secure enough to continue the program solo. Continue with clients who need the extra confidence until both of you feel that the client can handle the dog competently. Once training is complete, remind clients that you are always available should the dog's behavior regress, if further incidents occur, or if they simply have questions.

An unpleasant but sometimes necessary reason to terminate training is that a client will not comply with your suggestions. It is one thing to keep working with someone who is not practicing basic obedience exercises; that can be frustrating, but the worst that will happen is that the dog will not learn as well as he could have. It is another thing entirely to be lax about client compliance when dealing with aggression issues. For example, you may have a client who, despite your instructions, continually allows her dog-aggressive dog to be off-leash at the park, thereby putting other dogs in danger. You may have clients who never practice the exercises you have taught, and make excuse after excuse, despite your best attempts to help them make the process work.

It may not be in your nature to "get tough" with people, but the stakes are too high in these cases not to be direct and assertive. Inform your clients pleasantly but in no uncertain terms that if they do not begin to follow your directions regarding training and management, you cannot continue to work with them. The bottom line is: You should do what you can to support and encourage your clients, and be understanding that "life happens" and compliance may not be one hundred percent at all times. But sometimes you will need to put your foot down, and, in rare cases, put the other one down as well and walk away.

Part IV

What Do I Do If...

Solutions for Specific
Issues and Situations

What Do I Do If...

Wouldn't it be nice to have a personal advisor who would come along to all your aggression sessions? This section is my attempt to offer the next best thing. The situations described in these chapters are all things I have experienced in my own career. Chances are, if you train long enough, you will find yourself in similar situations.

Although it would be impossible to address each and every scenario that might arise, the ones that follow are common. Some, such as a client not realizing there is an aggression issue, or not realizing the extent of it, happen with alarming regularity. Having to recommend euthanasia for a dog because the aggression is so severe will hopefully be an uncommon event, but it does happen. Being bitten at sessions should be an infrequent occurrence if you are using positive, gentle methods and are adept at reading canine body language, but it is best to be prepared ahead of time, just in case. Other common issues addressed in this section include what to do if one person in the family is using harsh physical corrections, and what to do if a dog in your group class displays aggressive behavior.

19

What Do I Do If a Client is Being Physically Harsh with a Dog?

Most trainers get into this business because of a love of dogs. So it can be extremely challenging to sit in a client's home and hear that a dog is being physically handled in a way we would consider harsh, or even worse, to see it happening firsthand.

I once did a session where the client's husband was out of town. After we had been chatting a while, the woman confided that whenever the dog growled at anyone, her husband would beat him. Although this was not easy to hear, it was important information, as those disciplinary measures helped to explain why we now had a dog who bit people without warning. At another private session, I witnessed a client's two-year-old son kicking the dog with such gusto that, like magic, I somehow found myself holding a small boy a foot off the ground by his shirt collar! And despite my advocating positive training methods, I have had students now and then in my group classes who slapped or kicked their dogs.

Maintain Your Composure

So what should you do if a client or one of their family members is being harsh with the dog? (Here's a hint: lifting them off the ground by their shirt collar isn't the proper response.) Whether you are hearing about an incident secondhand or witnessing it yourself, try not to react emotionally or wear a negative expression. Yes, I know, it's extremely difficult not to look aghast and exclaim, "You did *what?!!*" But if you demonstrate visually or verbally that you are appalled, disgusted, or otherwise unhappy with what the client did, you will almost certainly cause that person to become defensive. Once that happens, the chances that you will be able to get your point across and convince the person to try alternate methods will have greatly decreased.

When a client relays information about implementing a less-than-positive disciplinary method, stay calm, maintain a placid expression, and ask, "How did that work for you?" Chances are it hasn't solved the problem, or you wouldn't be there. If the client responds that it has not resolved the issue, that's your opening to say, "Then let's try something different. After all, you wouldn't keep taking a medicine that didn't work, so why keep using a method that's not effective?"

State the Facts

Explain the difference between suppressing a behavior and actually solving the underlying problem. I like to use the analogy of my having a habit that annoyed you—let's say I bite my fingernails constantly without realizing it. If you slapped me each time I nibbled a nail, I'd stop immediately; but it wouldn't address the underlying emotional stress that caused the nail-biting in the first place. And chances are that my original nervous tension, now with the added stress caused by being slapped, would manifest in another, perhaps more distressing way. Another likely side effect of this "training process" would be that my feelings toward you would change from ones of warmth and affection to those of resentment and fear.

Create Camaraderie

How one treats their family members, whether they have four legs or two, is a very personal issue, and an emotionally loaded one. Softening your delivery can help. If the man in the family is the one being harsh with the dog, appeal to his manly side. Let's say an adolescent retriever is obnoxiously mouthing family members, leaving behind bruises and hurt feelings. The man's response when the dog mouths him is to force the dog to the ground, slam him onto his back, and stare him down until the dog stops struggling and looks away. The man proudly boasts that his method must be working, because the dog no longer mouths *him*. In that case, you might concur that yes, he is correct that the dog is not going to try mouthing *him* again. By agreeing rather than explaining why those methods are counterproductive, you create a moment where the client is open to listening, rather than becoming defensive. "But," you might then ask, "what about your wife and kids? They're not physically capable of doing what you did, and we need a method that works for everyone."

You would go on to gently explain that the stress of being rolled and held down translates to frustration on the dog's part. And who's left for the dog to take it out on? The wife and kids. Now, you might be thinking, why pander to the husband? Why not just tell him straight out that those methods are outdated and don't work? Because you want him to listen, and to be open to trying something different—and he won't be if you launch what he perceives as an attack on the way he's been behaving.

> If the person who is employing the harsh physical methods is not present at the session, try to schedule another appointment for a time when that person can be there. It is much more effective for the offending party to hear from a professional trainer, rather than secondhand from a spouse or parent, why the behavior must cease.

The "Alpha Roll"

The aforementioned technique of rolling the dog on his back—the "alpha roll"—is still, unfortunately, pretty popular. Chances are you'll come across clients who use it as their chosen method of discipline. Instead of looking disapproving, perk up and share that the alpha roll is actually a pretty fascinating subject. Explain that the technique originated after a scientist studied the behavior of wolves, but it was later found that even wolves don't actually force each other to the ground. One voluntarily submits out of respect for the other. You have now shared an interesting story rather than making the client feel badly. And, you would finish by explaining, that's the kind of leader everyone wants to be—one whose pack members follow out of respect, not fear.

Using this type of soft yet direct approach, along with showing clients what *to* do, should be sufficient to encourage family members to try less heavy-handed techniques. And it will be difficult for anyone to argue that the alternative methods you suggest don't work when you demonstrate them with good results.

~ * ~ * ~ *~ * ~ * ~ *~ * ~ * ~ * ~ *~ * ~ * ~ *

In the rare case that you observe a family member doing something that is actually cruel and abusive to a dog, contact your local animal services agency and report the incident.

What Do I Do If
I am Bitten During a Session?

A friend of mine, when asked if a particular dog bites, likes to respond, "If it has teeth, it bites." I couldn't agree more. If you work with dogs long enough, whether they are aggressive or not, there is a chance you will be bitten. Obviously, working with aggressive dogs carries an increased risk of injury. But if you use gentle training methods and are adept at reading canine body language, your chances of being bitten are much lower than if you use heavy-handed, physically coercive methods, or neglect to monitor body language carefully.

Prevention

Let's take a moment to discuss how being bitten might be avoided. If a dog is sending subtle warning signals your way, you should be able to recognize them and stop doing whatever it is that is making the dog uncomfortable. You would then defuse the situation, take a moment to reassess your protocol if necessary, and continue the session. For example, if you were working on a resource guarding issue and the dog growled, that would be an indication that you surpassed his threshold and a more gradual approach is needed. If you were to ignore his warning signals and keep approaching, chances are you might be bitten.

While reading signals and defusing potential conflicts are well and good, sometimes a dog will become extremely aroused very quickly. In those cases, there is a risk that the next bit of canine communication will be in the form of a teeth-to-skin telegram, with you as the recipient. The good news is that, even then, you still have the chance to avert a bite. In most cases, the best course of action is non-action: stand still, cast your gaze downward and to the side, and remember to breathe. This non-threatening posture will let the dog know that his message was received, so there is no need for him to pursue further action.

Swallowing Fear and Switching Gears

In some sticky situations, attempting to change the dog's mindset can help. Years ago, I met with Janet, Steve, and Vader, their three-year-old, ninety-five-pound male German shepherd. Vader was aggressive toward people. (Imagine that—with a name like Vader, you'd have thought he'd be a fluffy bunny!) Vader bit Janet and Steve regularly in a variety of situations that included their reaching to pet him if he was lying down, reaching toward him in the evenings once it was dark, walking across the floor in certain situations, and having the audacity to breathe the same air if Vader was in possession of a valued item. Vader had also bitten a few strangers for good measure.

I should mention that this dog should have been muzzled before I ever walked in the door. Due to a confluence of unfortunate circumstances (their misplacing Vader's muzzle, and my dog Soko having passed away a few days earlier, causing my brain to congeal into a lump of oatmeal—and yes, I should have postponed the appointment), Vader was footloose and muzzle-free.

Most of the session actually went quite well. Vader had not shown any aggression toward me, had been responsive to the training exercises, and the couple was pleased. Near the end of our alloted time, I was sitting in an overstuffed chair in the living room while Steve and Janet sat on the couch. Vader was lying between us. He suddenly stood up, placed one front paw on each arm of my chair, and pulled himself up to lean in close. He then growled in my face while showing off all his pearly whites. Imagine my surprise—one minute I was sitting back in a comfy chair with my bait bag of treats, pleased as punch about how well the session had gone, and the next, there was a large, threatening German shepherd in my face. Now, *there's* a Kodak moment!

I could not have been more frozen than I already was, and freezing was apparently not doing the trick. Vader wasn't showing signs of moving away any time soon, and I did not feel confident that the couple could remove him from my immediate vicinity without arousing him further and causing me to get bitten. So I switched gears. I visibly perked up and called his name brightly (well, as brightly as one can call "Vader"), using the same tone of voice as I had been using to precede verbal cues throughout our training session. I immediately followed his name with, "Sit!" Since Vader had a solid conditioning in obedience commands, and the dog training deities were smiling that day, my request immediately switched Vader from an aroused, potentially dangerous mode to one of *Oh, we're working now!* It was as if someone had flipped a switch. Once Vader was sitting, Steve put a leash on him, removed him to another room, and we discussed what had happened. Although freezing is your first line of defense, in cases where it doesn't work or isn't possible, switching the dog from an emotional mode to a cognitive one may help.

Bite and Release

Most bites are not vicious attacks, but single bites where the dog lunges in, bites once, and releases. Although this certainly constitutes an actual bite, it is also a warning; if the dog wanted to do more damage, he would have.

Sometimes a bite and release is of a defensive nature. The dog may be protesting being handled in a certain way, trying to stop an attempt to take something from him, or feeling threatened by your body language at close range. These types of bites, though they should not be downplayed, do not normally do much damage and may only leave bruising or slightly broken skin. On the other hand, the dog may deliver a confident bite with more pressure, and then release. And if the dog has poor bite inhibition, even a warning bite can result in puncture wounds.

Regardless of the amount of pressure, when a dog bites, once again, your best course of action is to take no action. That might sound counterintuitive, given that the dog has just bitten you. But we are talking about a single bite, not an all-out attack. Becoming still and remaining that way can be difficult under those circumstances, but you must train yourself to do so in order to stay safe. If possible, turn your body slowly to the side, avert your eyes, and stay quiet. Breathe. Your body language will broadcast to the dog that you pose no threat, so there is no reason to bite again. If the owner is present, calmly and quietly suggest that she put the dog on leash or remove him from the area. Remember that in this type of situation many owners turn into virtual zombies, standing with mouth open, frozen in place. It can help to use the person's name to get her attention, and then repeat your request.

Once the dog is safely secured, sit down with the owner and discuss what happened and why. This may be the first time the dog has bitten anyone, or it may be one more in a series of incidents. Either way, you now have first-hand knowledge of at least one thing that specifically triggers the dog's aggression, and how it manifests. Give the client a calm play-by-play recap so she understands why the dog bit.

The reason for the bite may or may not include something you did. You may feel shaken, embarrassed, or even angry. That's normal. But strive for a neutral tone of voice when sharing your assessment, rather than sounding as though you are upset or blaming the client. The owner is already distressed and needs guidance, not more fuel for the emotional fire. Discuss management protocols to keep everyone safe for the time being, and offer recommendations on how to proceed. Do not attempt any more training at the time, as the dog's arousal levels will still be high and chances are you will not be at your calmest, either. Later, when you feel more settled, reassess how to approach the issue, or whether you want to refer the case to a more experienced trainer. If you do refer, ask permission to go along and observe how the trainer handles the behavior.

Multiple Bites/Attacks

There is a world of difference between an incident where a dog bites once and releases, and one where the dog latches on and holds, inflicts multiple bite wounds, or grabs and shakes. The disparity lies not only in the extent of the damage, but in the intent. In most cases, a dog who sticks around to bite more than once is not simply saying, "Please leave me alone—I'm uncomfortable." That dog is taking the offensive. *It is a dangerous situation.* While it would be impossible to give advice as far as what to do in every case, the following are solid overall strategies that do not require the intervention of the owner:

1. As previously mentioned, your first line of defense is to stand perfectly still. This advice still applies in cases where the dog has bitten multiple times. However, if your non-action is not having any effect and the dog continues to attack, it is time to move on to other tactics.

2. If a dog has latched on to your hand or arm, press slowly with firm pressure *into* his mouth. That sounds counterintuitive, but if you pull away, you are virtually guaranteed physical damage. The pressure will sometimes get the dog to release. At the wolf rescue center I worked with, often a feisty four-footed resident would grab an arm and apply pressure but not release (this was usually a testing behavior). The pressure technique worked like a charm.

3. If you have a canister of SprayShield™ where you can easily reach it, spray it directly into the dog's face, aiming for the eyes and nose.

4. Grab any solid object within reach and get it between you and the dog. Or, use a soft object such as a wadded up shirt, and stuff it into the dog's mouth.

5. If the dog is wearing a leash, assuming you are physically able—and we are all capable of much more than normal when the adrenalin is flowing—pull the dog away from you by the leash, and with a straight, locked arm, hold him out of biting range until the owner can grab him.

6. If the dog is wearing a leash and all else fails, pull the leash upward so that at least the dog's front paws are off the ground (if you are strong enough, pull all four paws off the ground). The goal is to choke off the dog's airway. *This is an extreme defensive measure that should not be confused with anything you would ever do in a training session by choice, or under anything but the most dire circumstances.*

It is discomfiting to imagine doing anything unpleasant to a dog, even in the context of self-defense. But while this type of situation may never happen in your entire career, it is best to be prepared for the worst-case scenario.

Should the Bite be Reported?

I have heard some trainers ask whether, if bitten, they should report the incident. Frankly, I don't know of a single trainer who has ever done so, nor have I ever made such a report. Being bitten is understood to be a risk inherent to the profession. The one circumstance under which I would recommend reporting a bite is if the dog is truly dangerous and the client is obviously not taking the behavior seriously, thereby putting others at risk. Remember, if you seek medical attention at a hospital, you will be asked to provide contact information for the dog's owner. That information will then automatically be reported to the local animal control agency, so consider your answer carefully.

Regardless of the level of the bite and its cause, the best response is always to deal with the situation as calmly as possible, regroup, consider why the bite occurred, and learn from the experience.

21

What Do I Do If I am Working with a Client's Dog and a StrayDog Approaches?

Whether you train in a city, a suburban neighborhood, or a rural area, chances are that at some point, while working with a client's dog in public, you will encounter a stray dog. This is a potentially dangerous scenario, not only because the dog you are working with might be dog-aggressive, but because of the unknown temperament of the stray. Being prepared can help you to avoid a situation that is unsafe for both dogs, and possibly even litigious, should the client's dog be injured and you be held responsible.

An Ounce of Prevention

Have a safety preparedness discussion with your client before you begin to train outdoors. Explain that if a stray dog shows up, you will handle the situation. The owner's job is to keep her own dog safe. If her dog is a small one, she should pick him up and turn and walk away. If the dog is too big to lift, she should walk him away as calmly and quickly as possible.

Because people tend to freeze up in emergency situations, it's a good idea to practice ahead of time. Tell your client that whenever you say, "Grab your dog!" it means she should remove her dog from the area immediately as discussed. Practice the exercise on walks now and then to ensure that the owner becomes accustomed to performing the actions before they are actually needed. If a stray dog appears, chances are much higher that your client will comply with your instructions at once.

Don Your Supertrainer Cape

So how exactly should you deal with the stray while your client is ensuring her own dog's safety? It depends on the individual dog. If the stray does not appear threatening, your best course of action is to take a large handful of treats and toss them with an underhand motion behind the dog, scattering them as widely as possible. While the dog is intent on picking up each morsel, you and your client can safely retreat in the other direction. Another tactic for non-threatening dogs is to face the dog, draw yourself up to full height, and sternly say, "Go home!" while giving an authoritative wave of your arm. But use caution—if you're not sure whether a stray is friendly, don't chance increasing his arousal levels by becoming threatening yourself. The goal is to defuse the situation with as little confrontation as possible.

If a stray dog is moving toward you in a threatening manner and you are carrying SprayShield™, this is the time to use it (so long as the wind is not blowing in your direction). Spray it directly into the dog's face. It won't harm the dog, and should give you enough time to get to safety. If you are carrying an air horn, the sound may be enough to scare the dog off; it will also alert others if you need help. (Avoid using an air horn if your client's dog is noise-sensitive.) If necessary, pick up a nearby rock or other solid object and hurl it in the stray's direction, aiming for the ground next to the dog. This should be enough to scare the stray away, especially if you use your voice in an assertive manner along with it.

Threats to Your Personal Safety

The chances of a stray dog actually attacking you are slim, but it's important to know what to do if it happens. Chances are you will not be able to outrun the dog, and besides, running would only trigger the dog's chase drive and escalate his arousal levels. If there is a car nearby, climb up onto the roof and call for help. Perhaps the Trainer-on-the-Roof scenario isn't the most dignified, but it is immensely useful for keeping your limbs intact. If there aren't any cars or anything else close by to climb on, but there is a nearby gate or doorway, get yourself on the other side of it as quickly as possible. Then either find assistance or wait for the dog to leave.

But what if you can't easily retreat, and the dog is actually attacking you? Many safety manuals advise that if you cannot get away from an aggressive dog, you should curl up in a fetal position and cover your face. I relay this information because it is the accepted "right" thing to do, and is probably a very valuable tactic for children. There is obvious value in bearing the brunt of an attack on your limbs rather than on your face or torso. But unless the dog actually knocks you to the ground, I do not advise the fetal curl tactic. There is no way I would voluntarily surrender the advantage of an upright position if a dog were attacking me. In fact, I know very few trainers who would. Get a solid object between you and the dog if possible. Or, if you are holding a jacket or other soft item, stuff it in the dog's mouth. If there is no chance of retreat and no chance of using the aforementioned techniques, do whatever you have to in order to defend yourself and get out of the situation. Kicking is safer than using your hands or arms, as your legs are normally more protected, assuming you are wearing those thick jeans we discussed back in Chapter Ten. For women, the lower body is stronger than the upper— another reason to remain upright if you are a female.

No one wants to think about hurting a dog, but it is best to consider now what to do if the worst happens. In the event that you must defend yourself, you do not want to waste precious seconds wondering what to do.

Again, the likelihood of a stray dog attacking you is slim. The chances of a stray getting into a fight with a dog you are working with, especially if that dog is dog-aggressive, are higher. In the event that your client's dog is actually fighting with the stray, break it up (specific instructions for how to break up a dog fight are coming up in Chapter Twenty-three), get your client and her dog to safety, and then discuss what happened and why. Explain to your client how to keep her dog safe on walks when you are not there by carrying SprayShield™, an air horn, or a small folding umbrella that can be opened in the direction of the approaching dog. Above all, remember that the calmer you stay in any situation where a dog is highly aroused, the safer the outcome for everyone.

22

What Do I Do If
I Have an Aggressive Dog
in My Group Class?

Any dog who poses a danger to other dogs or people should not be allowed to attend a group class, unless it is specifically a "growl class" set up by an experienced trainer. Consider how you would feel as a student in an obedience class where, week after week, you were subjected to the presence of a dog who posed a potential threat to you or your dog's safety: You might wonder about the trainer's judgment in allowing a dangerous dog in class; you might discuss your feelings of resentment with other students; or you might simply drop out altogether. Afterward, you might share your feelings with others in the community. As a trainer, consider what that would do to your reputation.

You might feel that you are doing an owner a favor by allowing her to enroll her aggressive dog in class, but it's quite the opposite. In addition to the detrimental consequences for your other students, consider the effects that being in the class could have on the dog himself. Canine behavior patterns become more and more ingrained with practice. Threatening other dogs or people who respond by moving away builds the dog's confidence and reinforces the behavior. And sharing the same space with other dogs week after week can worsen a territorial dog's issues. In many cases, a group situation is actually counterproductive to modifying aggression issues.

As an instructor, you have a responsibility to your students. They expect you not only to teach and motivate, but also to ensure their safety and that of their dogs. Just as you wouldn't hold a class in the middle of the street with cars zooming by, you shouldn't conduct a class under *any* hazardous circumstances—and those include having dangerous dogs in class. This is not only an ethical matter, but is potentially a legal one if a bite incident occurs. Aggressive dogs should be seen in private sessions until they can be trusted to behave appropriately in a group environment.

Pre-Screening

Pre-screening dogs before the semester begins is one way to act as a responsible gatekeeper. Whether you chat with prospective students by phone or have them fill out a questionnaire online or via mail, be sure to include questions about the dog's experience with others. Ask whether he regularly spends time around unfamiliar dogs and people. If he has never met another dog, or has not been around many strangers, his reaction to them in a group situation might be one of fear or fear-based aggression; this information would alert you to keep a watchful eye during class.

Ask specifically whether the dog has ever bitten or threatened another dog or person. While the dog might not have actually bitten, a response might include, "He often lunges at other dogs." Perhaps no bite has occurred because the dog has always been on a leash when encountering other dogs. While that would theoretically prevent a bite in a class setting, you cannot guarantee that the owner will always have a secure grip on the leash or maintain a safe distance from the other dogs. And your students would probably feel unsafe with that dog present, for good reason.

You will not always get accurate assessments from owners about their dog's behavior. Some owners are in denial that their dog has an aggression issue at all, while others do not realize the extent of the problem. Then there are those who misinterpret their dog's behavior. For example, an owner might believe their dog is being protective of them when in reality the dog is afraid of people and the reactive display is his way of protecting *himself*. In that case, the dog might be dangerous even when he is not in close proximity to the owner—an important distinction for the trainer who attempts to demonstrate an exercise using that dog! Some owners believe their dog is a good candidate for group classes because he gets along with their other dog at home; but because the dog has not been exposed to unfamiliar dogs, the owner does not realize there is a potential problem.

If you feel at all hesitant about a prospective canine student during the pre-screening process, even if it's because you "have a feeling" but can't quite put your finger on the reason, meet with the owner before the semester begins. This should be a brief assessment, not an in-depth temperament test. Meet at a nearby park or other area where you are sure to encounter both dogs and people, so you can observe the dog's reactions firsthand. If the dog is extremely reactive, suggest private lessons until the behavior has improved to the point that the dog can be trusted in a group setting. If, despite your best screening efforts, you end up with a potentially dangerous dog in your group class, take the student aside as soon as possible and suggest private lessons instead. If you like, offer to apply the payment made for group classes toward private lessons.

Reactive Dogs in Class

Often you will have dogs come through your group classes who are not necessarily dangerous, but are simply reactive around other dogs or people. Determining the difference is largely a matter of experience. Your assessment will be based on a combination of the information given by the owner and your observation of the dog's behavior in the group. A reactive dog might bark, raise his hackles, or even growl or air snap if another dog approaches, but will not actually attack another dog. If the dog does not present a danger there is no need to ban him from class, but make sure students maintain a safe distance from each other at all times.

In a normal obedience class without reactive dogs, a good ratio is one assistant to every four to six dogs. When you have a reactive dog in class individual attention becomes even more important, so strive to have a higher ratio of assistants to dogs. This is not only a safety issue, but is also important to prevent other students from feeling slighted by the amount of time spent working with the reactive dog. Try not to have more than one reactive dog per class.

Ten Tips for Class Management

The following preventive measures should be taken whenever you have a reactive dog in class:

1.   Suggest to your students that they take their dogs for a nice, relaxing walk before class begins. This cuts down on the amount of energy the dogs have during class, which decreases arousal and, in turn, potential conflicts. This tactic is helpful in any class, but is especially important when reactive dogs are involved.

2.   Do a brief equipment check at the start of every class. Flat buckle collars must be fitted securely so they cannot slip over dogs' heads. What

type of training collars you allow is an individual decision, but a dog who is reactive toward others should not be wearing a choke chain or pinch collar (and certainly not an electronic—that is, shock—collar). A head halter such as the Gentle Leader® is a much better choice, assuming the dog is comfortable wearing it. If you recommend head halters, instruct owners on how to acclimate their dogs to them before the semester begins, and in class have them clip the leash to both the ring of the flat buckle collar and the ring of the head halter for added security. Be sure students understand how to hold the leash and that they must maintain a firm grip.

3.   Circle 'n' Sniff: This exercise can be done at the beginning of any class to help the dogs become more settled and less interested in approaching each other. It is especially recommended when there is a reactive dog or dogs in class. Owners should bring a bed, blanket, towel, or mat for their dog to lie on. These items will serve as markers for each dog's space. Begin with dog-owner teams positioned in a wide circle, each next to their own marker. On your cue, each dog and owner is to walk slowly to the right until they reach the next dog's spot. Once there, the dog should be allowed to sniff the marker. (Tell students to be attentive and to interrupt if their dog tries to mark the marker!) After five to ten seconds, give instructions to continue on to the next spot, and so on. Continue until all dogs are back at their starting positions.

The purpose of this exercise is to allow the dogs to check each other out through scent, rather than meeting in an up close and personal way, which can produce tension. A calmer state of mind not only reduces the chances of conflicts, but allows the dogs to absorb information more easily.

4.   Set rules at the start of the semester about maintaining a safe distance between dogs, and remind your students as needed. Even when entering and leaving the training area, a two-leash minimum distance should be maintained. During class, the reactive dog should be worked at a safe distance, that is, one that does not elicit a response. This should be easily accomplished if your class is held outdoors. If the training space is indoors and/or small, consider whether there is a way for the student to work just outside of the area. For example, if the class is held in a veterinarian's office or storefront with pane glass windows, the owner could practice with the dog outside but still see what is being taught. (If the space is *too* small, do not accept reactive dogs into class at all.)

If it is possible for two people to attend class with the dog, all the better: one person can stand close enough to hear and then relay your instructions, while the other works the dog at a distance. As his behavior improves, the dog can be worked gradually closer in to the rest of the class. If, despite your best efforts, you end up with two reactive dogs in class, they should be positioned as far from each other as possible at all times.

Note: For dogs who simply need to become habituated to the presence of other dogs, socialization is more important than learning skills perfectly. Be sure owners understand this, and do not feel badly if their dog is not progressing with the training exercises as well as other students.

5. Barriers can help dogs to remain non-reactive by blocking out the visual stimuli that contribute to arousal. Inexpensive yet effective barriers can be constructed using PVC pipe and fabric. As the dog becomes more comfortable, the owner can work with him just outside the barrier for short periods of time, with the eventual goal of no longer using the barrier at all.

6. If a student is having trouble maintaining a grip on the leash because the dog pulls or lunges, make it easier by tethering the dog to something stable. If you own or lease the teaching space, large metal eyehooks inserted into wall studs make for great anchors. In this type of scenario, the tether should be a coated wire cable (see *Resources*) that is clipped to the dog's collar, with the other end clipped to the eyehook; these come in a variety of lengths. Another option is to use a heavy cinderblock with an

eyehook screwed into it. In a situation where the reactive dog is a small one and the person is having trouble keeping hold of the leash, a hands-free waist leash can help. (See *Resources*.)

Note: Tethering can also be used for extra security. For example, when training at a park or other fenced area, a dog could be tethered to the fence with a long line as the owner works him on a regular leash—both are attached to the dog's collar.

7.   You and your assistants should always be alert for the first signs of stress in your canine students. Be particularly vigilant about keeping an eye on reactive dogs and those who are in close proximity to them. *Preventing a fight is much easier than breaking one up.* Watch for posturing such as freezing, a hard stare, raised hackles, or bared teeth. Listen for growling or barking. If you allow dogs to chew bones during class (such as peanut butter-stuffed bones to keep barkers quiet), keep an eye out for resource guarding.

If you notice a dog becoming stressed or reactive, suggest that the owner take him for a short walk and then return. If you see signs of potential conflict between two dogs, interrupt them. Get their attention by calling their names in a happy tone of voice or, if necessary, by clapping your hands. Then move the dogs away from each other or redirect them to other activities. Teach your students how to get their dog's attention rather than intervening in a way that might potentially escalate the conflict such as shouting at or jerking the dog (which might also result in a redirected bite). Once again, if you see behavior that is truly aggressive rather than reactive, remove the dog from class and suggest private sessions instead.

As well as monitoring dogs for posturing, watch for subtle stress signals. These may include lip-licking, yawning, turning away of the head and/or body, scratching, and leaning against or hiding behind the owner. Note these signals not only in the reactive dog, but in the dogs around him; sometimes other dogs will correctly assess the intentions of another dog before you can. Also, if you are teaching in a room with a tile or linoleum floor, look for small damp spots where the dogs have been standing; when dogs are stressed, their paw pads become damp.

> The Japanese have come up with an invention to detect canine stress. It consists of a patch that is placed on a dog's paw pads. When the dog's pads become damp from sweat secretions, the patch turns colors, like a mood ring. I can't help but envision a class instructor shouting, "Better grab Buddy, his strip's turned blue, he's about to blow!"

8. Teach your students to reward their dogs for checking in with them, and to keep the dogs busy between exercises while you are talking. This can be accomplished with simple exercises like attention and touch. The more the dogs are focused on performing skills, the less likely they are to become aroused and reactive. Keep explanations short and dogs active.

9. Manage activities so you don't have highly excited dogs in close proximity to each other. For example, if you were doing an exercise where owners call their dogs to them from across the room, you would not want to have six dogs all flying toward their owners at the same time in a small area. Depending on available space, have a few dogs at a time engage in a high-energy exercise while the others practice a more sedentary one, such as the down-stay.

10. Dogs are not the only ones whose safety you must consider. Some dogs are aggressive toward people; those applicants should have been pre-screened and rejected. But even a dog who is not normally aggressive toward people may inflict a bite onto a person due to a high state of arousal. For example, a student isn't paying attention to what her English bulldog is doing, and he pulls her toward a Jack Russell terrier. The terrier feels threatened; both dogs begin to posture and become aroused. As the owner reaches to grab her bulldog's collar, the terrier, now in a high state

of arousal, bites her. Maintaining a safe distance and following all the preceding rules will help to avoid this type of conflict.

In Case of Emergency

You must have a protocol in place in case a fight breaks out in class. If you have assistants, be sure they are informed as to how to intervene, as well as what to do if a dog attacks a person (although the latter scenario is much less common). Specific instructions for how to break up a fight can be found in the next chapter. These contingency plans should always be in place, and bear reviewing before the start of each semester. If a fight breaks out in class, in a calm yet urgent tone, ask that everyone hold on to their own dogs, then deal with the problem. If a dog attacks a person, do whatever is necessary in a steady, decisive manner to remove the dog from the area.

Growl Classes

For those dogs who have progressed in private lessons to the point of being able to start interacting with other dogs, and those who simply need frequent, supervised exposure to other dogs, growl classes are an invaluable resource.

Growl classes are specifically intended for dog-reactive dogs. The goal is that, over the course of the semester, they will become more comfortable with each other. Canine candidates for class may be reactive, but should not be truly dangerous. A growl class should only be taught by a confident instructor with many years of experience working with aggression. Unlike a regular obedience training class, in a growl class, assistants are an absolute must, as all dogs must be carefully supervised. Dogs are muzzled for safety at all times, and strict safety protocols are followed.

Growl classes are a great alternative for owners of dogs who are not yet appropriate for regular classes. They can help owners to feel less ostracized, since all the dogs in class are reactive, and the structured, supervised exposure and exercises can help the dogs immensely. (If you are interested in learning more about growl classes, see *Resources*.)

Next, we'll discuss how to break up a dog fight in as safe a manner as possible.

23

What Do I Do If I Have to Break Up a Dog Fight?

Whether it happens in a group class, a client's home, or out in public, you may find yourself in the position of having to break up a dog fight. Although this occurrence will be less common in private training situations—and even then, it should be rare—as always, it is best to be prepared.

Hands-Off Methods

Your first instinct upon seeing a fight might be to jump in and try to break it up yourself. As someone who still has scars from doing that very thing, I would encourage you to try a hands-off approach first. Following are a few options.

1. *Air horn.* Although air horns have already been mentioned, a more thorough description is in order. An air horn resembles a can with a small horn on top. When a button is pressed, it emits an ear-splitting sound that is extremely startling to humans and dogs alike. Upon hearing it, most dogs (and most people) will momentarily stop whatever they are doing, which gives you valuable time to intervene and get the dogs safely contained. Air horns can be found at boating supply stores and online. One caveat: That sound is likely to scare the heck out of all dogs in the vicinity, so if you are teaching a group class with a fearful dog in it, or your private client's dog has a fearful disposition, an air horn should not be your first choice.

2. *Spray away!* If there happens to be a water hose nearby—for example, when working in your client's back yard—turn it on full force and spray both dogs. Aim for their faces. You may also want to keep a canister of

SprayShield™ citronella spray handy. If you can intervene before the conflict escalates too far, SprayShield™ is worth a try. (Again, do not use the spray if you are downwind.) Bear in mind that once a fight has turned serious, spraying water or citronella may not help.

3. *APW extinguisher.* Another item to keep on hand in case of emergency is an air-pressurized water extinguisher. This option is more appropriate in a group class setting—private clients might be a bit alarmed to see you entering their home carrying something that looks like a fire extinguisher! The two-foot silver canister weighs 25 pounds and is filled two-thirds of the way with ordinary water, then pressurized with normal air. The spray is expelled with strong force. Spraying both dogs is likely to break up a fight, or at least produce a moment in which the dogs are startled, so that you can step in and defuse the situation. Avoid using regular fire extinguishers, as the chemicals may be harmful to dogs.

Whichever hands-off method you choose, if it succeeds in causing a break in the action, take the opportunity to remove the dogs to separate areas to allow their arousal levels to subside.

Hands-On Methods

In cases where hands-off methods are not enough:

1. If another person is available and both dogs are dragging leashes: You and the other person should each take hold of a leash and calmly move the dogs away from each other.

2. If another person is available but the dogs are not leashed: You and the other person should each grab one of the dogs by the hind legs, *high on the leg above the knee* (this lessens the chance of injuring the knee), and pull up so the dog's legs are off the ground—you should look as though you are holding a wheelbarrow. The legs must be held high enough that the dog cannot whip around and redirect onto you (a common occurrence when a dog is that aroused).

With each dog in wheelbarrow position, maintain a firm grip and walk backward, away from each other. Once you are at a safe distance, carefully place a leash on at least one dog and move him out of the area.

(If you can get both leashed, even better.) Then assess the damage and, if necessary, seek veterinary care. I cannot stress enough the importance of performing the leg-grabbing technique gently but firmly and with precision, as difficult as that might be in the heat of the moment. Although I have broken up many dog fights without injury to either dog, I have heard of a trainer breaking a dog's leg when attempting this technique.

3. If no one else is willing or able to help break up the fight, remain as calm as possible, and place whatever is handy between the dogs. This does not include your own limbs! Never place your hands or legs between fighting dogs. This common practice is almost guaranteed to result in injury to you, as is grabbing each dog's collar in an attempt to separate them. Something large, flat, and hard is ideal (if you bring a hardcover looseleaf binder or clipboard to class, grab it), but use whatever is handy.

If you teach group classes at the same indoor facility each week, consider keeping an item such as a large cookie sheet on hand, or better yet, a large, solid cutting board with pre-cut handles on both ends. (Some trainers prefer a thick wooden board with rope handles on each end.) Once you have positioned the item between the dogs, maneuver so you are moving one dog backward. This can be accomplished by walking into the dog's space with the item between you, while taking care that your body is to the side of both dogs, rather than between them.

If the training space has separate rooms, maneuver the dog into another room and close the door. If your space consists of one large, open room, while you have the item between the dogs, get someone to carefully place a slip lead over one dog's head as you wrangle the other, and then remove both dogs to safety.

4. You might want to keep a "breaking stick" on hand, particularly if you work regularly with bully breeds. Breaking sticks are designed to pry a dog's jaws open when they are locked on another dog, and are used frequently with pit bulls because of their jaw strength and tenacity. (Pit bulls do not actually have locking jaws—that's a myth—but you wouldn't know if it you were trying to pry one's jaws open!) The stick resembles a wooden dowel that is tapered at one end. It is meant to be inserted into the dog's mouth between the back teeth, and then turned to pry the jaws open. For ordering and detailed instructions, see *Resources* for Pit Bull Rescue Central's web site.

Some of the preceding measures may sound drastic. With careful management, hopefully you will never have to resort to using any of them. But take some time now to consider which products you will keep on hand, and if you teach group classes, which procedures you will review with your assistants.

What Do I Do If
the Client Doesn't Realize
the Dog has an Aggression Issue?

Sometimes the problems trainers are called in to address have nothing to do with aggression, but…surprise! It turns out there is an aggression issue after all. (A box of chocolates is *such* a nicer surprise, don't you think?) This scenario may occur when an owner is unaware of the dog's aggressive tendencies, knows but does not view them as problematic, or does not realize how potentially dangerous the dog's behavior has become.

The Tale of Thor

Nancy lives with her husband, twin five-year-old boys, and an eighteen-month-old male Rottweiler named Thor. Nancy had contacted me in the hopes of curbing Thor's habit of jumping on visitors. As you might imagine, most people did not appreciate a ninety-pound Rottie doing the full-body, happy-to-see-you greeting slam. Thor *was* actually happy to see visitors—there was no problem there, other than his poor manners.

As Nancy and I sat in the living room chatting, Thor lay at my feet, happily chewing the Kong® I'd brought along to keep him busy. I had stuffed a soft piece of chewy heaven into the small hole, which he was industriously trying to coax out. After fifteen minutes, as Nancy and I discussed Thor's poor manners and his artistic prowess (he had re-landscaped the backyard in the ever-popular "moon crater" motif), I noticed that the Kong® had been emptied. I reached down to refill it. That's when I simultaneously saw the whites of Thor's eyes and heard the growl that conveyed in no uncertain terms, "That's *mine*." Now, to my mind, this type of behavior falls into a category I like to call "Things that Could Have Been Mentioned."

I froze for a second, and without making eye contact, slowly withdrew my hand. I asked whether Thor ever guarded things from Nancy or other family members. She looked confused and asked what I meant. I clarified that I wanted to know whether Thor ever growled or showed signs of not being happy when approached if he was in possession of a chew item, a toy, or anything else. "Oh, that," she said dismissively. "He's always been a little grouchy around his food and bones, so we just don't go near him when he has something."

A discussion of resource guarding ensued, including an explanation of Thor's transition into adulthood and how its accompanying increase in confidence could result in an escalation of the problem. Without making it sound as though Thor was a "bad dog"—which he wasn't—or ignoring Nancy's original concerns, I stressed the need to modify the resource guarding behavior immediately, especially for the sake of the sons' safety. I assured Nancy that we would work on the greeting behavior as well and, in fact, we began to address both issues during that session.

Red Flags

Your tip-off that there is an aggression problem might not be as dramatic as a growl. A fast, hard glance as you reach to attach a dog's leash to his collar might indicate a handling issue. If a dog takes an offered chew item and retreats under the kitchen table instead of gnawing on it nearby, that's a red flag to ask about and perhaps even test for resource guarding issues. Of course, not every dog who takes an item away to chew has a guarding issue, but some do, and the owner may not even be aware of it.

Whatever the issue, it is important that you mention it. Take care not to offend the client with your phrasing—"Jeez, Buster just growled, why didn't you *tell* me he's got an aggression problem?"—but don't sugar-coat it or play it down, either. *Regardless of why the client originally sought help, no issue is more imperative to address than aggression.* A dog might jump on visitors, drag his owner down the street on walks, and grab things off the kitchen counter, but none of those things will be a deal-breaker as far as the dog staying in the home. A dog biting a person, however, is the first step down that dark road that often leads to a dog being given up and, sometimes, to euthanasia.

The Discussion

State the facts clearly and directly. If the aggression is directed toward family members, especially if there are children, discuss the potential threat to their safety and the importance of addressing the behavior immediately. If the dog is aggressive toward strangers or unfamiliar dogs, inform your clients that if the dog bites a person or injures someone else's dog and they are sued, they could lose their home and their homeowner's insurance, and the dog could end up being euthanized. Many owners do not take aggression issues seriously until it is too late, as demonstrated by the frantic calls trainers get after a serious bite has occurred. No matter the type of aggression, first and foremost, discuss how to implement a management program so everyone stays safe, and then outline a behavior modification program if appropriate.

The Sobering Six

Whenever your clients are not aware that the dog has an aggression issue, do not realize how serious it is, or don't understand its ramifications, sit them down and explain the facts clearly and without being accusatory.

1. Discuss the issue itself, explaining possible causes, the dog's subtle and obvious warning signals, and how the behavior might progress if left untreated.

2. Discuss the legal and personal ramifications should an incident occur.

3. Discuss management to keep everyone safe.

4. Discuss the overall treatment plan, and assure the client that you will address the initial concern as well.

5. Ask whether your client understands and is willing to work on modifying the aggression issue per your suggestions.

6. When you leave, congratulate yourself on having averted a possible disaster.

Next, we'll examine the options if an aggression issue is not resolvable.

25

What Do I Do If
an Aggression Issue is Not Resolvable?

In most cases, so long as your clients are willing to carry out your recommendations, their dog's behavior should be modifiable. But every now and then you may come across a dog whose behavior you feel cannot be changed, or a situation where it would not be safe for the dog to remain in the home. Before you share that information with the client, though, take a moment to review your level of certainty. If you have not had extensive experience with the type of aggression involved, or you are not one hundred percent sure that nothing else can be done, consider the following options.

Refer it Out

There is absolutely nothing wrong with telling a client that you feel a second opinion is warranted. After all, the prognosis could literally mean life or death for the dog. People seek second opinions for medical conditions, so why not suggest seeking one for a behavioral anomaly? Doing so in no way belittles your own skills or status. As a dog owner, I would have infinitely more respect for a professional trainer or behavior specialist who suggested seeking a second opinion than I would for one who seemed to care more about her own reputation and being able to fix the problem herself than she did about my dog.

If you are familiar with a behavior specialist in your area who handles aggression cases, and you feel confident in the person's abilities and comfortable with the methods used, refer the client. Another type of professional you could refer to is a Certified Applied Animal Behaviorist, or a Board Certified Veterinary Behaviorist. These specialists can be located through their respective organizations (see *Resources*). You may be lucky enough to find one in your area, but much of the time these services are provided long-distance.

Board and Train

If you are experienced with handling a particular type of aggression and feel that a circumstance in the home is contributing to the problem, boarding and training the dog can be an excellent solution. A board-and-train arrangement can jump-start progress with an aggressive dog whose owner does not have the time, leadership skills, or training finesse to get the dog over the initial hump. In other words, it is an effective way to get a foot in the door to change established behaviors.

As professional trainer and behavior specialist Valerie Pollard explains, "Board-and-train separates a dog from what is often an unbalanced relationship with the owner and gives him a chance to bond with the trainer and learn a new way of relating to the world. It can take a territorial, 'king-of-the-hill' dog away from his kingdom and put him in a place where he is 'no one,' which gives him a chance to learn in a healthy way so that when he goes back home it seems as if everything has changed." Of course, the owner must be instructed on how to work with the dog when he returns home so there is no backsliding.

Board-and-train can also sometimes work virtual miracles in cases where it seems there is no hope. Valerie relates the following story: "I used board-and-train once for two female dogs that were fighting terribly—they couldn't even be in the same area, and had put each other in the vet with serious puncture, tearing bites. I put them in a kennel in adjacent runs so that they were the only familiar thing to each other, and then we worked with them separately and eventually together. By the end they could be turned out together in the little run area, and also could heel together, down-stay next to each other, and perform other obedience skills together. I had the owner install runs in her yard that we still used for safety so they could continue the mindset of the kennel—that they were lucky to get out, and only under the direction of the owner."

As Valerie Pollard aptly notes, "The trick of successful use of in-kennel training for aggression is careful evaluation of the owner and the situation, and careful transition back into the home environment."

You can either board the dog at your own facility or partner with an established kennel. Another approach would be to visit the client's home a few times each week to work with the dog, without the owner present. You would, in effect, be doing board-and-train by using the client's home as the boarding facility. After a number of sessions (for example, a package of ten), you would meet with the client to discuss the dog's progress, demonstrate behaviors that were taught, and explain how to continue working with the dog. If you do not wish to offer board-and-train in any form, but feel that this type of training would be helpful, refer the client to another trainer who offers the service. Be sure to get a recommendation from a trusted source, or observe the trainer in action before you refer anyone.

~ * ~ * ~ * ~ * ~ * ~ * ~ * ~ *

In cases where you feel certain that the dog's issues are not resolvable, it is time to have a talk with the client. There are really only three options for dogs whose aggression issues are so severe that they pose a threat to the safety of other dogs or people: management, rehoming, and euthanasia.

Management

In situations where the client absolutely wants to keep a severely aggressive dog no matter what, management is the only choice. In the aforementioned scenario with the two female dogs, the owner was advised to use lifelong management to prevent fights. For your clients, management measures will depend on the individual situation. For example, if the dog's aggression was directed toward other dogs on walks, an effective management plan would include using a muzzle and possibly a head halter whenever the dog was in public.

A dog who poses a threat to visitors must be managed very carefully. In a household that consists of adults only, placing the dog in a locked room or outdoor containment area whenever friends are expected will ensure everyone's safety. But when children are involved, there really is no such thing as one hundred percent reliable management. Kids leave doors and gates open, and forget instructions; sooner or later there is bound to be an accident.

I have had clients whose dogs posed an extreme threat to people, yet they were determined to keep the dog. Extreme management measures were taken, such as building an escape-proof pen in the back yard with a padlocked perimeter fence around it so no one could stick their hands through the fencing or let the dog out. If owners are willing to go to those extremes, and to take the dog out regularly under careful supervision and spend quality time with him, this type of management can work. But if the dog is relegated to living out his life in solitary confinement in what amounts to a chain-link prison, it is time to assess the dog's quality of life.

Rehoming

Ah, that mythical ranch where dogs who have lost their homes romp and play, destined to live out their lives in a state of blissful contentment, watched over by kindly caregivers. Wouldn't it be nice if that ranch existed? It does—in the minds of many owners who have to give up their dogs. Unfortunately, rehoming a dog with an aggression issue is not that simple.

In some cases, dogs with certain types of aggression issues that are beyond behavior modification *can* still be rehomed. Specifically, if a dog is fighting with another dog in the home but gets along well with other dogs, rehoming is a viable solution.

If a dog is aggressive toward children, he could, theoretically, be sent to live in a childless home—but even so, the world beyond those four walls is filled with children. If the adopter was permanently housebound, did not have visiting kids or grandkids, and had a way to exercise the dog in places where no children are allowed, it would be the perfect situation—somewhat unlikely, but perfect. Short of that, even if a childless person is willing to adopt a dog who is aggressive toward kids, the situation must be assessed extremely carefully so that no child will ever be placed at risk.

Liability may be involved when adopting out a known biter. In many states, if a dog bites someone after being placed into a new home, the original owners can still be held responsible.

Many owners believe that aggressive dogs can simply be handed over to rescue centers. After all, the purpose of a rescue group is to take in dogs who can no longer stay in their homes, and to then adopt them out, right? Having been involved in rescue work for many years, I can assure you that the vast majority of legitimate rescue organizations will not accept an aggressive dog. If they did, they would very possibly be stuck caring for that dog for the rest of his life. Can you imagine a family looking for a dog to adopt, and the rescue group showing them around, saying, "We have *this* lovely dog who was found as a stray and loves everyone, *that* one gets along fabulously with other dogs, and…oh, right! Here's Chester—he's bitten three people! How about him?"

Although there are some rescue organizations that will take in aggressive dogs and either care for them for life or attempt to rehabilitate them, it's not the norm. And unfortunately, some who accept them end up placing those dogs, still aggressive, into new homes, where the cycle is perpetuated. *Ethical rescue groups will not knowingly adopt out aggressive dogs.* In cases where it would not be safe to adopt the dog out, explain to your clients in a gentle but direct manner why giving the dog to a rescue group or rehoming him is not an option.

Euthanasia

Discussing the possibility of euthanasia with owners is one of the most difficult tasks a dog trainer will ever face. With luck, and good assessment and training skills, the number of times you will have to suggest it will be few and far between. But in those cases where all other options have been exhausted and the dog poses a serious threat, euthanasia is the only choice left.

When talking about euthanasia with a client, it is exceedingly important that you be sensitive and compassionate. The decision to put one's dog down is one of the hardest anyone will ever make—and the client is the one who must make it. Your role is to present a prognosis and an overview of the options. First, discuss management. If management is not possible or would not be a reliable choice in the particular situation, explain why. Assuming that rehoming or surrendering the dog to a rescue group are not options either, explain why not. Clarify that giving the dog to the local shelter is not recommended either. If a shelter is aware that a dog has bitten they will euthanize him—and not disclosing the bite history would be unethical, as someone else would very likely be bitten.

Gently mention euthanasia as an option, and even steer the client toward that choice, but do not *tell* the client to put the dog down. It is important that owners come to this conclusion on their own, rather than having it forced upon them. Without other options, the vast majority of your clients will come to the appropriate decision.

One tactic I have found helpful in cases where it would be unsafe for the dog to stay in the home is to ask clients to imagine that instead of taking action, they do nothing—and then the worst happens. For example, you are there because the dog has delivered level three bites to the child on two separate occasions. "Imagine how you would feel," you might say to the mother, "if you did nothing and Dakota ended up biting Billy severely. How would you live with that?" The same scenario applies to dogs who are fighting with each other: How would the person feel if one dog badly injured or even killed the other, when the person knew it could have been prevented? This line of reasoning not only makes a legitimate point, but allows the person to feel less guilty about taking the required action.

Many times when clients enlist your services, they already know deep down that euthanasia is the appropriate choice. What they are seeking is your professional assurance that it is the right thing to do. That reassurance gives owners a feeling of permission to go ahead with the process, knowing they have done all they can. I can relate, although the situation was not a behavioral one: When my dog Soko became ill, we did everything we could for her. In fact, we kept her alive with a good quality of life for almost a year more than would have otherwise been possible by rearranging our home and our work schedules for her comfort. Finally, with indecision lingering in my heart, we brought her in to be euthanized. Our veterinarian examined Soko and then, seeing my distress, said kindly, "You went so much further than most people would have gone. You did everything you could. It's time." His words meant a lot to me. They removed that nagging doubt that there was something else I could have done. They absolved me of guilt. And that is sometimes your role when visiting a client who already knows that "it's time."

Offering Support

Spend as much time with your client as necessary, and be as supportive as possible. I know some trainers who even offer to accompany clients to the vet's office when their dog must be euthanized. I cannot personally handle the emotional aspect of that, but it is a kind and noble gesture. Find your own comfort level, but be available to support your clients emotionally. And be sure to take some time afterward to decompress. Dealing with these sorts of issues can be terribly stressful for trainers. If talking about it helps, find a friend, colleague, or therapist, and let it out. Get a relaxing massage, go home and smother your own dogs in love and tummy rubs, or do whatever else gives you peace of mind.

Speaking of peace of mind, next we'll discuss ways you can avoid burnout.

26

What Do I Do
to Avoid Burnout?

Any career, from dentist to driving instructor, can eventually lead to burnout. The repetitive nature of doing the same thing day in and day out can result in boredom, fatigue, frustration, anger, and eventually, apathy. Many people continue to do their jobs anyway, albeit with a certain level of resignation, or they move on to another career. But if your job happens to be the thing you are passionate about in life—which for many trainers happens to be dogs—the added emotional component can intensify the problem.

When dog trainers burn out, we begin to dislike handling phone inquiries, wish clients would cancel, have less patience at training sessions, and have less enthusiasm for the job overall. We may become irritable with those around us, become lethargic, or even fall into a state of depression. At that point some trainers take a break and eventually return with a new enthusiasm, while others leave the profession permanently.

Reasons for Burnout

Frustration and irritability run high in customer service professions, and it's no different for dog trainers. After all, what trainers really do is to train *people* to train their dogs. Although some simply tire of teaching the same skills over and over, or giving the same behavioral advice for what seems like the thousandth time, the biggest contributor to burnout for dog trainers is the emotional wear and tear of dealing with clients. It can become frustrating to return to a client's home time after time to find that no one has practiced with the dog, and downright irksome to deal with owners who constantly ignore your advice or yes-but you every step of the way.

A lack of owner cooperation is bad enough when you are working with everyday obedience and manners issues, but noncompliance can be terribly frustrating when you know that the owner's actions—or lack of them—will very likely determine life or death for the dog.

In aggression cases, the stakes are high for everyone involved. When a dog has attacked a person or another dog, the owner may be fraught with frustration, anger, guilt, or embarrassment. Emotions become even more intense when rehoming or euthanasia are necessary, as the owner faces the loss of her beloved companion. Trainers often end up playing the role of advisor, family peacekeeper, and source of emotional support. Clients vent their frustrations on us, call us between training sessions for advice, and sometimes even cry on our dog-hair-covered shoulders.

Being the compassionate dog lover you are, you may become emotionally involved in and even distraught over your cases. There is a saying among animal rescuers that "you can't save every one" and, unfortunately, that applies to aggressive dogs as well. But being cognizant of that fact and remaining unaffected are two very different things.

Dealing with complex behavior cases also demands much more of a time commitment than handling typical training issues. You will spend more time on initial phone conversations, preparation for sessions, history-taking, post-session notes, follow-up with clients, and in some cases, composing assessments for the client's veterinarian. That investment of time and energy can become arduous, especially if the majority of your practice consists of aggression cases.

Try Something New

By suggesting that you "try something new," I do not mean that you should dye your hair purple or get a tattoo. What I am recommending is that you learn and practice new and different techniques to work with aggressive dogs. In addition to helping you serve your clients better, it will help to keep the job challenging and appealing. You could attend local trainer roundtables and exchange ideas on how to work with specific types of aggression. Or perhaps there is a technique you have used in other situations, but never thought to apply to aggression cases. Maybe it's a matter of thinking outside the box entirely by incorporating a complementary therapy such as Ttouch or flower essences. Even though you are still working with the same issues, taking a fresh approach can help to reawaken that spark of fun and creativity.

Get a Booster Shot of Enthusiasm

A great way to refresh your passion for training is, ironically, to attend a training conference such as the annual one offered by the Association of Pet Dog Trainers (APDT). Eagerness to learn and a wild enthusiasm for training fairly radiates off the attendees, and is completely contagious. You're bound to make a few new trainer friends, get a chance to relax at dinners and fun events, and learn fresh, new techniques to try out when you get home. If finances prohibit you from attending a conference, you can purchase CD-ROMs of the event (see *Resources*), or buy some new DVDs or books that take a new approach to aggression or illustrate different techniques than those you have been using.

Strive for Balance

An important aspect of avoiding burnout is to maintain a balance in your caseload. Seeing dogs with various types of issues is infinitely easier on the psyche than dealing solely with aggression. If your practice is such that working with aggression issues constitutes the majority of your business, add something different.

What about teaching a puppy class? Sure, it's completely at odds with your specialty—that's the point. Puppy classes are lighthearted and fun. When I taught them years ago, no matter how bad my mood might have been before class, I always felt much lighter and happier afterward. (I'm convinced that bottling the joy that comes from being around puppies could solve 99 percent of human depression cases.) If not puppy classes, consider teaching tricks training or a CGC (Canine Good Citizen) class—see the American Kennel Club's website, www.akc.org, for more information.

Other Activities

An alternative to teaching other types of classes is to participate in them with your dog. You could try fun sports like Rally O (a kinder, gentler version of competition obedience), freestyle (dancing with dogs), agility, or tracking, to name a few. Or, if your dog has the temperament for it, consider doing therapy work; all those joyful smiles at seeing you and your fur-kid can go a long way toward balancing the stress you encounter in your everyday work. Go hiking, jogging, or swimming with your dog, or just spend some quality time together at a local park.

Another great way to avoid burnout is to get involved in non-dog-related activities. Yes, Virginia, they do exist. So many trainers I know have lives that revolve around dogs and training, and that's pretty much it. Find other interests. A trainer I know who specializes in aggression issues is also a black belt in Tae Kwan Do. The martial art not only offers a completely different experience from what she does in her everyday dog-related work, but the physical component is a great stress-reliever. The required mental focus means that rather than thinking about her work or feeling tense, she must be completely present and in the moment.

Although any type of exercise or sport is useful, the activity need not be physical. Whatever your interests, indulge them. Take a class in something you've always had a longing to try. Learn French. Join a book club, or any group with common interests. Plan social activities with friends, and mark the dates on your calendar just as you would training appointments—they're that important. You might not think your schedule will allow it, but making time for outside activities now will ensure that you don't have plenty of time on your hands later due to feeling too burned out to work.

Relaxation

There are many paths to relaxation. Some people thrive on activity, while others unwind by engaging in more sedate pursuits. Doing yoga, tai chi or qigong can soothe your mind and revitalize your energy, as well as being good for your body. Meditation is another excellent practice, and one that has many proven health benefits. Being constantly on the run and dealing with stress can weaken your body's defenses; studies have shown that meditation, among its many benefits, can actually strengthen your immune system. And the peace and relaxation you will find by meditating or engaging in any of the aforementioned activities will help you to deal more effectively with stressors that arise in and out of the training arena.

Of course, your idea of down time might simply be watching a movie or becoming absorbed in a novel. Whatever it is, give it the same importance as you do your training sessions; it's all about balance.

Talk it Out

Some people naturally handle stress more easily than others. But no matter what your level of ability to cope, it can be helpful to talk about what's bothering you. If you are lucky enough to have a partner or a friend who is willing to listen, take advantage of the opportunity. It can be especially helpful to share and vent if the person is a trainer, as he or she will certainly relate to what you're going through. If you don't have a confidante and you are experiencing high levels of stress due to the emotional aspect of the work, consider seeing a therapist. I realize that might sound extreme, and I don't mean to suggest that all trainers need therapists! But there may come a time when you are less capable of dealing with the stress alone, especially if aggression cases constitute the majority of your practice. A good therapist will not only listen and offer advice, but will give you the tools you need to cope with difficult psychological situations throughout your career.

Take Some Time

If at all possible, take a vacation now and then. I have to confess that advice is hypocritical coming from someone whose travels consist of teaching seminars and who hasn't had a real vacation in years. I'm self-employed and my boss is a slavedriver! But don't you do it. If you haven't taken a vacation in a while, you might have forgotten how effectively it can recharge your batteries and give you a more balanced perspective.

If a vacation is out of the question, at the very least, take day trips. A change of scenery can go a long way toward relieving stress. If there's something you love to do—for example, shop—combine the two in a shopping trip to a nearby scenic town. If you like wine, visit a winery. If you have a friend whose company you enjoy, arrange to go together. Just don't make day trips to other training facilities, and if you're on an airplane, don't get roped into talking about dog training with your seatmate for the whole flight!

~ * ~ * ~ * ~ * ~ * ~ * ~ * ~ *~ * ~ * ~ * ~ * ~ * ~ * ~ *

Although you might feel that you have to take on as much work as possible for financial reasons, plan for the long term. You will eventually crash and burn if you do not take some of the aforementioned steps now. Striving for balance, talking it out, and being involved in activities outside the dog training world can go a long way toward keeping your enthusiasm for your work high. If not for your own benefit, do it for all those clients and dogs who will benefit from your assistance in the future.

27

Three Wishes

I hope you have found the information in this book useful. You should now have a better understanding of the ins and outs of working with aggression issues, and how to go about gaining further education and experience.

My three wishes for you as you pursue your work with aggression cases are that:

1. No matter how many methods and techniques you learn, you will always trust your own instincts and intuition above all else.

2. You will always remember that somewhere under those aggressive displays are "good dogs" who are simply in need of some understanding and assistance. Treat them and their owners with compassion, and if you find yourself becoming hardened, take steps to avoid burnout.

3. Regardless of how far you go in the field and what level of success you achieve, you will keep learning and networking with other trainers. Supporting each other, rather than viewing each other as competition, will not only help more dogs to stay in their homes, but will advance our profession as a whole.

Resources

~*~*~*~*~*~*

Resources

Books and other resources by Nicole Wilde are available through Phantom Publishing (www.phantompub.com.) Many of the other books, videos, and DVDs are available through Dogwise (www.dogwise.com), Tawzer Dog Videos (www.tawzerdogvideos.com), amazon.com, and your local book retailer.

BOOKS and DVDs

Aggression

Aggression in Dogs
Brenda Aloff
Collierville, TN: Fundcraft, Inc., 2002 ISBN 1-59196-073-8

Dogs are from Neptune
Jean Donaldson
Canada: Lasar Multimedia Prod., Inc., 1998 ISBN 0-9684207-1-0

Fight! (dog-dog aggression)
Jean Donaldson
San Francisco, CA: Kinship Communications, 2004 ISBN 0-9705629-6-9

Mine! (resource guarding)
Jean Donaldson
US: Kinship Communications, 2002 ISBN 0-9705629-4-2

"Clicker Training for Aggression" DVD
Donna Duford

"Biting" DVD
Dr. Ian Dunbar

"Doggy Play, Social Behavior, Friendliness, Fighting and Biting" DVD
Dr. Ian Dunbar

"Abandonment Training" DVD
"Modifying Aggression in Different Types of Dogs" DVD
"The Different Faces of Aggression" DVD
"Training Difficult Dogs" DVD
Trish King

Applied Dog Behavior and Training (volumes 1-3)
Steven R. Lindsay
Ames, Iowa: Iowa State University Press, 1999-2003

The Cautious Canine (booklet)
Patricia B. McConnell, Ph.D.
Black Earth, WI: Dog's Best Friend, Ltd., 1998 ISBN 1-891767-00-3

"Dog-Dog Aggression in & Outside of the Home Environment" DVD
Patricia B. McConnell, Ph.D.

Feeling Outnumbered? (managing a multi-dog household)
Patricia B. McConnell, Ph.D. & Karen B. London, Ph.D.
Black Earth, WI: Dog's Best Friend, Ltd., 2001 ISBN 1-891767-06-2

Feisty Fido: Help for the Leash-Aggressive Dog
Patricia B. McConnell, Ph.D. & Karen B. London, Ph.D.
Black Earth, WI: Dog's Best Friend, Ltd. 2003 ISBN 1-891767-07-0

*Aggressive Behavior in Dogs: A Comprehensive Technical Manual
for Professionals*
James O'Heare
Canada: DogPsych Publishing, 2007 ISBN 978-0973836929

Clinical Behavior Medicine for Small Animals
Karen L. Overall
St. Louis, Missouri: Mosby, 1997 ISBN 0-8016-6820-4

Click to Calm: Healing the Aggressive Dog
Emma Parsons
Waltham, MA: Sunshine Books, Inc., 2005 ISBN 1-890948-20-9

"Cujo Meets Pavlov!" DVD
Kathy Sdao

"Fighting Dogs: Family and Strangers" DVD
"Sibling Rivalry" DVD
Pia Silvani

"C.S.I. Crime Scene Investigation" DVD
(includes info on setting up growl classes)
Cheryl Smith

"Defensive Handling for Trainers & Instructors" DVD
"Possession Aggression" DVD
"Small Dogs, Big Issues" DVD
"Yowser! A Guide to Defensive Handling Techniques" DVD (This title available directly through www.suesternberg.com)
Sue Sternberg

Body Language

Dog Language: An Encyclopedia of Canine Behavior
Roger Abrantes
Wenatchee, WA: Dogwise Publishing, 2001 ISBN 978-0966048407

"Dog Language" DVD
Roger Abrantes

Canine Body Language: A Photographic Guide
Brenda Aloff
Wenatchee, WA: Dogwise Publishing, 2005 ISBN 1-929242-35-2

How to Speak Dog
Stanley Coren
New York, NY: Fireside, 2000 ISBN 0-684-86534-3

"The Language of Dogs" DVD
Sarah Kalnajs
www.bluedogtraining.com

The Other End of the Leash
Patricia McConnell, Ph.D.
The Ballantine Publishing Group, 2002 ISBN 034544678X

"Reading Between the Lines" DVD
Patricia McConnell, Ph.D.

On Talking Terms with Dogs: Calming Signals
Turid Rugaas
Wenatchee, WA: Dogwise Publishing, 2006 ISBN 1929242360

"Bite-O-Meter" DVD (This title available through www.suesternberg.com)
"How a Dog Tells You he is Going to Bite you Long Before he
Actually Does" DVD
Sue Sternberg

Breed Information

The Encyclopedia of the Dog
Bruce Fogle, DVM
New York, NY: Dorling Kindersley, 1993 ISBN 0-7894-9149-5

Paws to Consider
Brian Kilcommons and Sarah Wilson
New York, NY: Warner Books, 1999 ISBN 0-446-52151-5

Genetics and the Social Behavior of the Dog
John Paul Scott and John L. Fuller
Chicago, IL: University of Chicago Press, 1965 ISBN 0226743381

The Perfect Match: A Dog Buyer's Guide
Chris Walkowicz
New York, NY: Macmillan, 1996 ISBN 0-87605-767-9

Complementary Therapies

Animal Reiki
Elizabeth Fulton and Kathleen Prasad
Berkeley, CA: Ulysses Press, 2006 ISBN 1-56975-528-0

Bach Flower Remedies for Animals
Helen Graham & Gregory Vlamis
Tallahassee, FL: Findhorn Press, 1999 ISBN 1-899171-72-X

Homeopathic Care for Cats and Dogs
Don Hamilton, DVM
Berkeley, CA: North Atlantic Books, 1999 ISBN 1-55643-295-X

Four Paws, Five Directions: A Guide to Chinese Medicine for Cats and Dogs
Cheryl Schwartz
Berkeley, CA: Celestial Arts, 1996 ISBN 0890977904

Natural Healing for Dogs and Cats
Diane Stein
Freedom, CA: The Crossing Press, Inc., 1993 ISBN 0895946149

Getting in Ttouch with Your Dog
Linda Tellington-Jones
North Pomfret, VT: Trafalgar Square, 2001 ISBN 1570762066

The Well Connected Dog: A Guide to Canine Acupressure
Nancy Zidonis and Amy Snow
Larkspur, CO: Tallgrass Publishers, LLC, 1999 ISBN 0-9645982-4-8

Fear Issues

The Cautious Canine (booklet)
Patricia B. McConnell, Ph.D.
Black Earth, WI: Dog's Best Friend, Ltd., 1998 ISBN 1-891767-00-3

"Frightened Fidos" DVD
Pia Silvani

Help for Your Fearful Dog
Nicole Wilde
Santa Clarita, CA: Phantom Publishing, 2006 ISBN 0-9667726-7-9

"Working with Fearful Dogs" DVD
Available directly from www.phantompub.com

Health and Nutrition

Canine Neuropsychology
James O'Heare
Canada: Gentle Solutions, 2005

Dr. Pitcairn's Guide to Natural Health for Dogs and Cats
Richard H. Pitcairn, DVM, Ph.D. & Susan Hubble Pitcairn
Emmaus, PA: Rodale Press, Inc., 1995 ISBN 0-87596-243-2

Holistic Guide for a Healthy Dog
Wendy Volhard and Kerry Brown
New York, NY: Howell Book House, 2000 ISBN 1582451532

Learning Theory

How Dogs Learn
Mary Burch and John Bailey
New York, NY: Howell Book House, 1999 ISBN 0876053711

Excel-erated Learning
Pam Reid, Ph.D.
Oakland, CA: James and Kenneth, 1996 ISBN 1888047070

"Learning Theory 101" DVD
Kathy Sdao

Legal Considerations

"Avoiding Liability when you Train, Shelter or Adopt Out" DVD
Kenneth Phillips, Esq.
www.tawzerdogvideos.com

Dogbitelaw.com
Articles on legal issues regarding dog bites, as well as resources for
trainers.

Medical Influence on Aggression

"Genetic and Environmental Factors Affecting the Health of Today's
Dog" DVD
Dr. Jean Dodds

Applied Dog Behavior and Training (volumes 1-3)
Steven R. Lindsay
Ames, Iowa: Iowa State University Press, 1999-2003

Clinical Behavior Medicine for Small Animals
Karen L. Overall
St. Louis, Missouri: Mosby, 1997 ISBN 0-8016-6820-4

Tawzer Dog Videos
Health Issues section has DVDs on vaccination, thyroid connection to
behavior issues and more.
www.tawzerdogvideos.com

Also, do an internet search for Jean Dodds and aggression for links to pages
regarding the connection between thyroid levels and aggression, and
vaccination and aggression.

PRODUCTS

APDT Conference CD-ROMs
www.netsymposium.com

Assess-a-Hand (and Sue Sternberg booklets/DVDs)
www.greatdogproductions.com

Breaking Sticks
Pit Bull Rescue Central
www.pbrc.net/shop/bsticks.html

The Dog Trainer's Business Kit (CD-ROM)
(liability contracts, forms, handouts)
Phantom Publishing
www.phantompub.com

Gentle Leader, Easy Walk Harness and other products
Premier Pet Products
1-888-640-8840
www.premier.com

Muzzles
Morrco Pet Supply
www.morrco.com

Snoot Loop head halter
www.animalbehavior.com

Tethers
www.dogwhispererdvd.com/products

Waist Leash
1-888-363-2818
www.buddysys.com

LIABILITY INSURANCE

Business Insurers of the Carolinas
(Offers insurance specifically to APDT members)
1-800-962-4611

The Hartford Insurance Company
1-888-253-4940

EDUCATION

Companion Animal Sciences Institute (online courses)
www.casinstitute.com

Legacy Canine Behavior and Training (Washington)
Terry Ryan
www.legacycanine.com

Peaceable Paws (Maryland)
Pat Miller
www.peaceablepaws.com

Marin Humane Society Canine Behavior Academy (California)
415-506-6280
www.marinhumanesociety.org/behavior/CBA.html

Raising Canine (telecourses)
www.raisingcanine.com

San Francisco SPCA Academy for Dog Trainers (California)
415-554-3095
http://www.sfspca.org/academy/index.shtml
DogAcademy@sfspca.org

ORGANIZATIONS

Association of Pet Dog Trainers (APDT)
www.apdt.com

Certified Applied Animal Behaviorists
Animal Behavior Society
www.animalbehavior.org

Veterinary Behaviorists
American College of Veterinary Behaviorists
www.dacvb.org

Other Books by Nicole Wilde
Available at www.phantompub.com

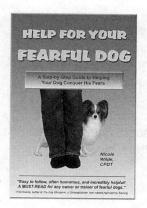

A comprehensive guide to the treatment of anxiety, fears and phobias. Written for trainers, other canine professionals, rescue/shelter workers, and owners. Covers causes and prevention; body language; skills and techniques for owners; skills to teach dogs; treatment plans for 15 specific fears; complementary therapies. Studies, photos, illustrations, and step-by-step instructions.

Everything new and aspiring trainers need to get their business up and running, as well as tips for established trainers. Getting an education; setting up a business; advertising, including website tips; running group classes; in-home sessions; phone tips; safety tips; trainer etiquette; products and tools. Extensive updated Resources section.

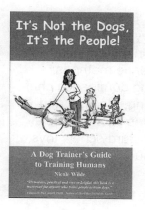

Training dogs is the easy part! Now learn to hone your human-training skills. Family dynamics; group class dynamics; working with kids; dealing with difficult personality types from Argumentative Al to Bland Betty, Needy Nita to Know-It-All Ned.

(This title is also available as an audio CD.)

More Books by Nicole Wilde

Everything trainers need to know about teaching private lessons. Selling single sessions versus packages; scheduling tips; phone scripts; history questionnaires; structuring lessons; designing protocols; contracts and handouts you can use with your clients; handling inconsistent clients; what to do if you are bitten; discussing euthanasia; more.

New second edition of the classic guide to wolfdogs, also known as wolf hybrids. Revised and updated with new photos and diagrams. What to consider when considering a wolfdog; legalities; containment; nutrition; training; compatibility with your human and four-footed pack; and more! A must-read for anyone considering sharing their life with these incredible yet challenging animals.

The title says it all! Everything you need to know about wolfdog training and behavior: training with positive, gentle methods; behavior issues including dominance challenges, guarding, jumping, digging, and chewing; important issues such as socialization and enrichment; sturdy chew toys; veterinary care; fear issues; myths versus reality.

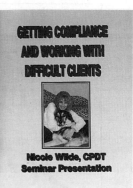

The Dog Trainer's
BUSINESS KIT
CD-ROM

Contracts - Forms - Handouts

For PC or Mac (Word, Pages, and .pdf files)

This new, easy-to-use CD-ROM contains contracts, handouts, and more to help you stay organized and professional, and to free up your valuable time so you can do what you do best—train dogs and their people. You can easily add your own business name/ logo to the forms, change, add, or delete text, or use them as is.

Client Information Form: 5-pg. Advance Questionnaire.
Behavioral Questionnaire: 5-pg. form for aggression issues.
Contracts: Private Lessons, Group Classes, Board and Train.
Phone Intake Forms: 2 per page, use in notebook or stack.
Client Sheet: 1-page form for sessions/use as intake form.
Homework/Activities/Progress Chart
Veterinary Cover Letter/Behavioral Assessment
Handouts: Crate Training/Housebreaking, Exercise, Introduction to Clicker Training, Leadership Program, Nutrition, Principles of Positive Training, Kong Stuffing, article "Leadership Versus Dominance."

www.phantompub.com